A
Gendered
Choice

For Anna and Elliot, my inspiration each and every day

A
Gendered
Choice

Designing

and

Implementing

Single-Sex

Programs

and Schools

David W. Chadwell
Foreword by Jim Rex

CORWIN
A SAGE Company

For information:

Corwin
A SAGE Company
2455 Teller Road
Thousand Oaks, California 91320
(800) 233-9936
Fax: (800) 417-2466
www.corwinpress.com

SAGE India Pvt. Ltd.
B 1/I 1 Mohan Cooperative
    Industrial Area
Mathura Road, New Delhi 110 044
India

SAGE Ltd.
1 Oliver's Yard
55 City Road
London EC1Y 1SP
United Kingdom

SAGE Asia-Pacific Pte. Ltd.
33 Pekin Street #02-01
Far East Square
Singapore 048763

Printed in the United States of America

Library of Congress Cataloging-in-Publication Data

Chadwell, David W.
A gendered choice : designing and implementing single-sex programs and schools/ David W. Chadwell.
    p. cm.
Includes bibliographical references and index.
ISBN 978-1-4129-7259-8 (cloth)
ISBN 978-1-4129-7260-4 (pbk.)

    1. Single-sex schools—United States. 2. Single-sex classes (Education)—United States. 3. School management and organization. I. Title.

LB3067.4.C43 2010
371.821—dc22   2009035717

This book is printed on acid-free paper.

09   10   11   12   13   10   9   8   7   6   5   4   3   2   1

Acquisitions Editor:	Carol Chambers Collins
Associate Editor:	Julie McNall
Editorial Assistant:	Brett Ory
Production Editor:	Eric Garner
Copy Editor:	Gretchen Treadwell
Typesetter:	C&M Digitals (P) Ltd.
Proofreader:	Theresa Kay
Indexer:	Wendy Allex
Cover Designer:	Rose Storey

Contents

List of Tables

Foreword

Every now and then, a rare thing occurs. The right person comes along at the right time and takes full advantage of an opportunity to bring about rapid and substantive change. David Chadwell was that person in 2007 in South Carolina.

I had just been elected as State Superintendent of Education and had won (the only Democrat to win a statewide office) on a platform of educational reform that included a promise to create a choice-driven public school system. Two months into office, I visited a single-gender middle school program that I had heard rave reviews about from parents in Columbia, South Carolina. Dent Middle School had a number of options parents could choose from for their sons or daughters, but the most popular were the single-gender "academies" that had been pioneered at Dent.

I was immediately impressed by the excitement and commitment I saw that day, exhibited equally by students, teachers, administrators, and parents. At the center of this dynamic and unique learning community was the young man who had designed and implemented the program, but who was also obviously the continuing energy source for the other faculty and whom the students, faculty, and parents looked to for direction and, yes, inspiration.

This constantly moving, encouraging, smiling, and teaching energy source was, of course, David Chadwell. Without David's knowledge, within a week I talked to his district superintendent—Dr. Steve Hefner, one of the most creative and visionary public school administrators in our state. I asked Steve if he would be selfless on behalf of his state and his profession and allow me to make an offer to David to become the first person hired to work in the newly created Office of Public School Choice at the South Carolina State Department of Education. Viewing that I would owe him a debt not to be paid in this lifetime, Steve said yes. I was then able to convince David, beginning the summer of 2007, to become the first person in America to be hired as a statewide facilitator for public school single-gender programming.

Public school choice options must be made available to parents if we are going to meet the needs of all students. Of course, public school choice options need to be fully accountable and fully accessible. For school districts, single-gender education is a choice option that can address specific needs of the student population, blend with other school-based initiatives, be implemented quickly, and cost very little.

I have just completed the second year of my four-year term and I have watched with amazement as David Chadwell has engaged an entire state, and an entire profession, in the process of understanding both the advantages and the limitations of single-gender education. I have also watched as an incredible number of schools (at last count, over 200) have adopted single-gender choice programs vaulting South Carolina into national and international prominence as the leader in the number of public school single-gender programs (half of the programs in America are in South Carolina).

In my opinion, no one in America, or in the world for that matter, has amassed as much practical, successful knowledge and experience in the implementation of public school single-gender programming as has David Chadwell. In less than two years, he has worked directly with hundreds of teachers and hundreds of schools, and indirectly with thousands of students and their parents to create a level of momentum and acceptance that is unprecedented. This book, *A Gendered Choice*, is not only an invaluable guide and resource for those interested in learning more about single-gender education; it is an equally valuable and insightful resource for those who wish to understand better how America can successfully reform its public school system in the early twenty-first century.

As I said at the beginning of this foreword, David represents a rare combination of intellect, charisma, persistence, and passion that made him the right person at the right time in South Carolina to move public school choice forward through his remarkably successful advocacy for single-gender education. He also reminds us all that we have remarkably talented people in our American classrooms who are ready, willing, and able to lead in the transformation of American public education. As an author, he continues both that leadership and that transformation.

—Jim Rex, PhD
South Carolina State Superintendent of Education

Preface

We never educate directly, but indirectly by means of the environment.

—*Democracy and Education* (John Dewey, 1916)

Public school single-gender education is sprouting up across the United States as well as the world. However, until now, there has been no practical source on how to create a single-gender program. That is the purpose of this book: to help educators create quality single-gender programs. This book is about bringing an old idea back to public schools, but with a different face: the new single-gender programs are not a re-creation of the old single-gender schools. Rather than a theoretical book examining the merits of single-gender choice, this guidebook tackles the practical aspects of considering, creating, and sustaining excellent programs that allow girls and boys to learn separately.

ORGANIZATION OF THE BOOK

This book is divided into three sections—Considering, Designing, and Implementing Single-Gender Programs—in order to serve three different but overlapping audiences: If you are just considering single-gender programs, then you might want to start with Part I and work your way through the book sequentially. If you have decided to create a program, a brief look at Part I would be helpful to get the big picture, and then a systematic read of Part II would work well. If you have a single-gender program currently in operation, then you will probably want to start with Part III, and then return to specific chapters of interest in Part I and II depending on the particular issues within your school and community.

This book is designed as an aid and strives to be as practical as possible, while also providing theoretical support to points offered. To this end, each chapter contains a planning tool. The planning tool highlights main points from the chapter and provides an opportunity for the reader to reflect on these points. A substantial Resources section is also provided so that planners can have starting points and examples. All of these resources may be revised as readers deem necessary for their own situation.

Part I explores the issue of gender within education in the context of the twenty-first century. Chapter 1 presents four different lenses through which gender and education can be viewed. While I believe gender is an important aspect for educators to consider and respond to within their classrooms, schools, and districts, both positive and negative arguments and data are presented for the reader to consider. Awareness of both sides of the current gender debate within education will serve all those who are interested in single-gender education and the issue of gender differences. Chapter 2 presents the current landscape of single-gender education, including the demographic information about current single-gender programs and data gathered from national studies. Administrators frequently need this kind of data to support their interest in single-gender programs. In Chapter 3, the arguments against single-gender education are analyzed, as presented by the American Civil Liberties Union (ACLU) and National Organization for Women (NOW); all educators interested in, pursuing, or currently involved in single-gender education should be aware of their opposition. Chapter 4 addresses frequently asked questions in terms of socialization, planning, and instruction.

Part II is about designing a single-gender program. Each chapter walks the reader through a different component of creating a program and is good preparation for discussing the program with other educators, parents, and community members. Chapter 5 offers steps the reader can take in creating a rationale for the single-gender program, followed by several different structures that can be used depending on the specific rationale. Chapter 6 systematically describes and explores the practical implications of the Federal Regulations of October 2006. Chapter 7 then looks at the different constituents and how to best communicate with each: administrators, teachers, parents, students, and board members. Chapter 8 examines ways to build community within the single-gender program and across the school. Chapter 9 suggests ways that a single-gender program can be implemented at different cost levels; many readers may not be aware that a single-gender program can be accomplished at minimal cost.

Part III of the book is about implementing the single-gender program. Far too often, new programs are brought into a school only to fall apart the next year. The reasons vary from lack of leadership, teacher turnover, or inconsistent results. By the end of Part III, the reader should be able to put together a one- to three-year plan for implementing a single-gender program in a school or district. Chapter 10 provides a variety of professional development paths and opportunities. Again, it should not be assumed that professional development must cost large sums of money. In many cases, the timeline of implementation dictates the cost. Chapter 11 suggests ways that administrators can gather data to evaluate their single-gender program. Program review is required by the federal regulations, and using data to inform instruction is also an important part of professional development. Chapter 12 addresses the most common causes of abandonment of a single-gender program and provides suggestions to sustain a program. Certainly, these issues are not unique to single-gender programs, but they are worth examining for their bearing on the debate surrounding single-gender education.

Acknowledgments

O ver twenty years of discussions with parents, educators, and students are involved in the writing of this book. Whether exploring the dynamics of one's rights, respect, and responsibilities with college students, creating an inquiry project about the *Titanic* with third graders in the media center, or designing a middle school program in China, choice has always been at the heart of my educational endeavors. I am grateful to those peers, educators, and professors who gave me the opportunities to try something different, supported me in the process, and challenged me to examine my beliefs.

Special thanks to David Mallery for his faith that someone with a philosophy background could be a good teacher, and to Plymouth Meeting Friends School for giving me that chance.

Appreciation is due to the educators in Richland School District Two who work at the highest levels to bring a multitude of learning options to their students. I am grateful to the parents of the first class of the TWO Academies who had faith that what we were creating would be good for their child, to Charlene Herring for giving me a chance to collaborate on this adventure, to Jennifer Richter for working with me in its creation, and to the teachers and students for being patient with us as we made our way.

Jim Rex knew public school choice was needed, and single-gender education could be a catalyst of change. I am honored and humbled to be a part of his team to improve education.

Abigail James encouraged me to put the ideas on paper. Without her push, I would not have started the writing process.

South Carolina teachers and principals deserve medals for their commitment and passion as they work to create single-gender programs for their students.

Wanda Lincoln and Janet Kahler labored over the text to make my thoughts something others could use and understand. I never would have found clarity without their insights.

Carol Collins and Brett Ory helped in keeping this book on track.

Finally, thank you to my family for their understanding every time I said, "Not now, Daddy is working on the book." And to Amy for always keeping balance in our lives.

About the Author

 **David W. Chadwell** is the coordinator for single-gender initiatives within the South Carolina Department of Education. He works with schools across the state at all stages of implementing single-gender programs. He is also a consultant to principals across the country as they work to create single-gender programs and train their teachers. His comments on single-gender education have appeared in multiple media sources including MSNBC, ABCNews On-line, *New York Times Magazine*, *Education Week*, *Education Next*, *USA Today*, National Association of Elementary School Principals, and multiple state and local newspapers. In 2004, he helped start the first all-day middle school single-gender program in South Carolina. His career in education has taken him from a private Quaker school in Philadelphia to an international school in Tianjin, China, to public schools in Columbia, South Carolina. He received his master's degree in teaching from the University of South Carolina and his master's degree in philosophy and social policy from The American University. Readers can contact David through his Web site www.chad wellconsulting.com.

Introduction

Defining Single-Gender Education

Choice is opportunity. The choice of single-sex education is affirmative action for the sexes.

—Peter Meyer (2008)

On March 16, 2008, I received the following email from a parent:

> I have an 11-year-old daughter who is in sixth grade at XX in XX County. My daughter is gifted, introverted, sensitive, and has hit puberty and middle school—it's not a good mix! My daughter has always loved school and did fine in elementary. As soon as she hit middle school, I've watched with my heart breaking how her quiet, intelligent, sensitive, confident nature is being eroded by boys picking on her. It is especially hard in our society for a female to be quiet and intelligent and confident, and the boys in her middle school seem to already have that sense of "we need to put her in her place," and I see her struggling so much to the point where she hates school now. I do not even know what to teach my daughter anymore—do I keep teaching her to be herself, as I always have, and suffer the constant pain of rejection and insults and being "different," or do I teach her to be a "typical" female to fit in and suffer the constant pain of never being who she really is? (Personal communication, 2008)

On that same day, I read the following comment from Elena Silva, Senior Policy Analyst of Education Sector:

> But the link between gender and learning is weak. And the assumption that separate schools for boys and girls will make schools and districts better for students is way off the mark. (Silva, 2008)

1

This is the world of single-gender education, where stakeholders hold widely varying views about gender as an issue in education. There are parents asking for help with their children, teachers reaching out for other ways to reach their students, and students finding avenues of success that may not have been available a few years ago. And, there are policymakers making categorical statements on both sides of the issue. Throughout this book, the terms *single-gender* and *single-sex* are used interchangeably. Both terms are commonly used within schools and the media.

Single-gender education occurs when boys and girls are taught in separate classes during some or all of the school day. This can be a single-sex campus: an all-boy school or an all-girl school. This could also be a "dual academy": a coed school where boys and girls are in single-sex classes for the entire day. The other form of single-gender education involves a coed school with single-sex classes held during part of the day.

This book is written for administrators, teacher leaders, or parents who are interested in bringing a single-gender format to their public school or to create a public single-sex school. The issues involved with public single-gender education for schools, dual academies, or classes are similar. As such, this book is designed as a resource for each of these groups.

The majority of entry points into single-gender education are single-gender classes that are begun within coed schools. Educators involved in starting an all-girl or all-boy school will find multiple points of support throughout this book that are unique to the gendered aspect of their school. However, aspects related to starting a school, regardless of gender or specific charter school issues, are not addressed. The focus of this book is on the gendered aspects of single-gender programs.

The program organization of public single-gender education varies. For whole school or dual academies, all classes are single gender. In coed schools, single-gender classes could be core academic classes, such as mathematics, science, social studies, or English language arts. Or, the single-gender classes could be related arts, cocurricular or encore classes, such as physical education, art, music, or theater. In addition to or instead of academic class periods, a designated time of day may be single gender, such as breakfast, lunch, recess, or after-school activities. Or, in some cases, all classes and times are single gender, even though the larger institution is coed.

For a program to be designated as single gender, boys and girls must attend separate classes. These classes must be completely voluntary for the parents of students enrolled. Students cannot be forced to remain in a single-gender class if their parents do not want them to be in a single-gender class. We will be examining legal issues later.

SOME BASICS

It's worth making three fundamental points about single-gender programs before exploring the details of philosophy, program design, and implementation.

1. Public school teachers are responsible for teaching the state standards of their own state. In coed and single-gender classrooms, boys and girls must be taught and held accountable for the same set of state standards. Teachers cannot change the standards or decide which part of the standards to teach to boys and which to teach to girls, nor can less rigorous versions of classes be taught to one gender or the other.

Thus, in a single-gender program, the difference is not what is taught, but *how* the state and district standards are taught to boys and girls. The practice of using different instructional strategies to deliver a lesson or meet a standard with different populations of students is commonplace. The same math lesson will be taught differently in classroom A than classroom B because the students are different, whether those classrooms are coed or single gender. The background knowledge of students will be different, the questions that students ask will be different, and the pace at which the students understand the material will be different and will require different emphasis, clarification, or reteaching. Teachers *should* teach differently to different students. The same premise exists within single-gender classrooms.

2. Single-gender schools and classes are designed and designated as single-gender classes; they are not coed classes that happen to end up as single gender because only boys or only girls happened to enroll.

3. Finally, and perhaps most self-evidently: Teachers of coed classes teach both boys and girls. Understanding boys and girls better and learning about educational strategies that may better meet their needs is beneficial for all teachers.

PART I

Considering Single-Gender Education

Teachers, parents, and community members are slowly becoming more comfortable talking about gender-specific learning. Conversations are always interesting and charged, often going from personal experience to stereotypes. In this section, we will look at gender as part of the educational reform puzzle.

> *The best part of being in single-gender classes is being able to branch out and be okay with who you are.*
>
> —Fifth-grade girl

> *The best part is that you learn more when you are in single-gender classes.*
>
> —Seventh-grade boy

> *One of my best experiences is that there is increased participation. Students of both genders are not afraid to speak out and classroom discussions and activities are better.*
>
> —Elementary school teacher

5

1

Gender Makes a Difference in the Classroom

But it is not about simply separating the sexes, said Wilmette [Illinois] District 39 Supt. Glenn "Max" McGee. "It's about understanding how boys and girls are different, and then differentiating your instruction to reach them."

—*Chicago Tribune* (Banchero, 2006, sec. 4)

Gender cannot be ignored as an issue in education. The question isn't *whether* gender should be raised as an issue in public schools, but instead, *how* it should be raised. A growing body of research (Baron-Cohen, 2003; Deak, 2003; James, 2007, 2009; Kimura, 1999; Sax, 2005; Wilhelm, 2002) suggests there are important considerations about the differences in the ways boys and girls learn.

However, dealing with gender differences in the classroom is neither simple nor clear-cut. Effective educators know that the boys and girls in our classrooms have individual strengths and needs. Many schools already promote differentiated instruction to help teachers meet the needs of their students. Districts provide special education, and federal civil rights laws ensure that each student's unique needs are met. New technology enables school systems to deliver content to students in engaging ways and helps students access information in much more interesting ways. Some may ask, what more can the education establishment do? With all the resources teachers already have to meet the needs of students, why bring the issue of gender differences into the mix? The answer is that gender matters, and understanding gender differences can help students learn and teachers teach.

In the United States during the last several years, particularly since the federal government issued regulations in 2006 that modified Title IX and officially sanctioned single-gender classes and schools, many schools and districts have addressed the gender issue by instituting single-gender programs. The programs vary, and not one system fits every situation. But, regardless of variation, single-gender classrooms and schools are being implemented across the country.

As with most educational policies, there is controversy. At the time the federal guidelines were first issued, many groups and individuals voiced support for, and opposition to, allowing single-gender classes and schools. The debate continues on editorial pages of newspapers, during school faculty meetings, and among parents. Alice Ginsberg, Joan Shapiro, and Shirley Brown (2004), in their book *Gender in Urban Education,* highlight the issue: "Does gender equity mean the same things as being gender blind—that is, treating boys and girls exactly the same? Or does it mean paying closer attention to gender differences?" (p. 1).

Should I consider a single-gender program for my school?

Take a moment to consider your level of agreement with the following statements to determine your entry point into the conversation of gender.

- I believe students can perform better than they do now.
- I think that we, as part of the educational field, are not academically meeting the needs of our boys and/or girls.
- I think teachers can address the social needs of boys and girls better in single-gender classes.
- I think that the opposite gender negatively influences the behavior and performance of students.
- I think hormones play an important role in how boys and girls behave.
- I think there are some hard-wired differences that are important in the classroom.

STARTING POINT: EXAMINING GENDER INFLUENCES

Educators are certainly familiar with gender differences. They interact with boys and girls in the classroom every day, and most have heard about the "boy crisis" in achievement over the last several years. They are familiar with recent books on strategies for teaching boys and girls.

A balanced debate of gender in education includes four factors:

1. Data on student performance by gender

2. Socialization into male and female roles

3. Hormonal influences

4. Biological brain differences, often referred to as hard wiring

No one factor is more important than the others; they are simply ways to start the conversation about single-gender education. Certainly, they are not inclusive of all issues related to gender, and there is potential for overlap. But, for educators, these topics lead to observations about their own experiences and they stimulate thinking about how different students learn.

STUDENT PERFORMANCE

Can single-gender programs enhance student performance? Can they help teachers teach students more effectively? Teachers, administrators, and researchers are always looking at achievement and behavior data in classes and schools to improve learning results.

The first guiding questions are: How do boys and girls perform in relation to each other? Is there, in fact, a gender-based achievement gap in schools, districts, or states?

Take, for instance, the *Education Week* report, Diplomas Count 2008, which breaks down 2005 graduation rates (Table 1.1):

Table 1.1   2005 Graduation Rates by Gender and Ethnicity

	Males	Females
All Students	67.8	75.3
African Americans	48.2	61.3
Hispanic	52.0	62.7
White	74.3	79.8

Source: *Education Week*, 2008.

Based on these data, there is a gender difference in graduation rates across the United States. The difference exists across racial subgroups and is widest between African American girls and boys. Pedro Noguera (2008) summarizes:

> Throughout the United States, Black males are more likely than any other group in American society to be punished (typically through some form of exclusion), labeled, and categorized for special education (often without an apparent disability), and to experience academic failure. (p. xvii)

While schools and communities are working to address this gap, single-gender classes may be a format where these efforts can reap better rewards. As educators and as a nation, we cannot simply accept graduation differences within the public education system.

Often, educators will look at the performance by gender on the National Association for Education Progress (NAEP) report, often called the Nation's Report Card. The change over time for fourth-grade and eighth-grade boys and girls follows a similar trend (see Tables 1.2–1.5 on pages 10–11). Boys and girls are improving on a very similar path (U.S. Department of Education, 1996, 1998, 2000, 2002, 2005, 2007).

In reading, there is an approximately 10 percentage point difference between the number of boys and girls who perform below the basic score at the eighth-grade level (see Table 1.3). Looking further back, boys have made progress: The difference decreased from 13 percentage points in 1992 to 9 percentage points in 2007. This is good news. However, girls consistently outscore boys at the proficient and advanced levels of reading. In mathematics, the performance of boys and girls is almost identical at every level (see Tables 1.4–1.5). In fact, the percentage of boys and girls who score at the below basic level are parallel each year. (For both reading and math, basic indicates students who have "partial mastery" of the expected knowledge, proficient indicates students who demonstrate "solid academic performance," and advanced shows students with "superior performance." Those students not scoring at least at basic are at the "below basic" level [U.S. Department of Education, 2008].)

NAEP data point to success for both boys and girls. After all, both boys and girls are improving in mathematics and reading. The gender gap in mathematics is essentially nonexistent, and the gender gap in reading is decreasing. As such, the story could go that there is no gender-based performance gap. In fact, this is the claim made by The American Association of University Women in its report *Where Girls Are* in May 2008:

> Drawing from educational indicators from fourth grade to college, this report examines gender equity trends since the 1970s. The results put to rest fears of a "boys' crisis" in education, demonstrating that girls' gains have not come at boys' expense. Overall,

Table 1.2   Student Performance on NAEP, Reading Grade 4, by Gender

Percent of Students At or Above Each Achievement Level for Reading in Grade 4, NAEP								
	Below Basic		At or Above Basic		At or Above Proficient		Advanced	
Year	Male	Female	Male	Female	Male	Female	Male	Female
1998	45	40	55	60	25	30	5	7
2002	41	35	59	65	26	33	5	8
2005	41	34	59	66	27	33	6	8
2007	38	31	62	69	29	35	6	9

Source: U.S. Department of Education, Institute of Education Sciences, National Center for Education Statistics.

Table 1.3   Student Performance on NAEP, Reading Grade 8, by Gender

Percent of Students At or Above Each Achievement Level for Reading in Grade 8, NAEP								
	Below Basic		At or Above Basic		At or Above Proficient		Advanced	
Year	Male	Female	Male	Female	Male	Female	Male	Female
1998	36	21	64	79	23	37	1	3
2002	30	21	70	79	26	36	2	3
2005	34	24	66	76	24	34	2	3
2007	32	23	68	77	24	34	1	3

Source: U.S. Department of Education, Institute of Education Sciences, National Center for Education Statistics.

Table 1.4   Student Performance on NAEP, Mathematics Grade 4, by Gender

Percent of Students At or Above Each Achievement Level for Mathematics in Grade 4, NAEP								
	Below Basic		At or Above Basic		At or Above Proficient		Advanced	
Year	Male	Female	Male	Female	Male	Female	Male	Female
1996	39	39	61	61	20	19	3	2
2000	35	38	65	62	25	20	3	1
2005	20	21	80	79	37	33	6	4
2007	18	19	82	81	41	36	7	4

Source: U.S. Department of Education, Institute of Education Sciences, National Center for Education Statistics.

Table 1.5   Student Performance on NAEP, Mathematics Grade 8, by Gender

Percent of Students At or Above Each Achievement Level for Mathematics in Grade 8, NAEP								
	Below Basic		At or Above Basic		At or Above Proficient		Advanced	
Year	Male	Female	Male	Female	Male	Female	Male	Female
1996	40	42	60	58	23	21	4	3
2000	38	38	62	62	26	23	5	4
2005	32	33	68	67	30	27	6	5
2007	29	30	71	70	33	29	8	6

Note: Observed differences are not necessarily statistically significant. Totals might not add up to 100 percent due to rounding.

Source: U.S. Department of Education, Institute of Education Sciences, National Center for Education Statistics.

educational outcomes for both girls and boys have generally improved or stayed the same. Girls have made especially rapid gains in many areas, but boys are also gaining ground on most indicators of educational achievement. (p. 3)

Despite the apparent clarity of the report, however, it was met with swift disagreement. As one *USA Today* (2008) editorial opined:

The facts show that gender gaps start to emerge in elementary school and widen in middle school. Over the past thirty years of federal testing, girls' advantages on verbal tests have widened while the boys' advantages in math have narrowed. Girls end up graduating from high school at higher rates, earning far better grades and reaping most of the academic honors. This trend continues into college—the key to economic success in today's economy—where women are earning 62 percent of associate's degrees, 57 percent of bachelor's and 59 percent of master's. (Yes, university, para. 4)

NAEP is a useful gauge of educational performance. However, principals and teachers from across the country continue to report that boys are doing poorly academically when compared to girls, and that boys have more discipline referrals than girls. The data that seem to really matter to teachers and parents are the performance of students in their own schools, rather than on national standardized tests.

NAEP data are only part of the story about gender; individual state data provide a more detailed picture of what is happening with our boys and girls. In South Carolina, for example, students take the Palmetto Achievement Challenge Test (PACT) in Grades 3–8 (see Table 1.6). From 2005–08 there is a consistent gender achievement gap on the percentage of students scoring Below Basic on the English Language Arts portion of the exam, with boys running behind by between 8 and 14%. Boys are simply not performing at comparable levels to girls.

Table 1.6   Data From South Carolina State Report Card, 2005–2008

South Carolina: Percent of Students Scoring Below Basic in English Language Arts						
	3rd Grade	*4th Grade*	*5th Grade*	*6th Grade*	*7th Grade*	*8th Grade*
Female	9.60	14.35	16.90	23.68	21.15	21.50
Male	17.28	23.03	27.25	36.93	35.58	33.68

Source: South Carolina Department of Education, 2005–2008.

Looking at state report cards from South Carolina, New York, Illinois, and Washington—states that were picked as samples from the southern, northeastern, midwestern, and western regions of the country—it becomes apparent that there is indeed an achievement gap by gender that is pervasive across the country (see Tables 1.7–1.9). Results from other state assessments show a similar pattern to those of South Carolina, with the percentage of boys not meeting basic levels of achievement consistently higher than the percentage of girls who are underperforming.

Educators should ask themselves why this gender achievement gap exists, and review their own classroom, school, district, and state data. Skeptics may argue that data can be found to support any position. However, given the undeniable gender gap across the country, shouldn't we start looking at education and instruction through a gender lens?

SOCIAL DIFFERENCES

Of course, there are other factors to consider, apart from the evidence of academic test scores. Some single-gender educators argue that boys and girls should be schooled separately in order to provide an environment that encourages full participation and opportunity to express opinions without the influence of opposite-sex students. They believe that in a classroom free of boys, girls will have the chance to be the leaders and speak their opinions without fear of being laughed at by the boys. Also, in single-gender classrooms, girls, they claim, are not overly concerned about their appearance in relation to the males. Many find the atmosphere liberating. Conversely, boys have the opportunity to be themselves in a single-gender class without worrying that girls will think they are "dumb" when giving an answer or worrying about getting in trouble because the girls complain about them.

Supporters also argue that single-gender classes allow teachers to focus on either boys or girls and create an environment that promotes students' learning. Text selections, video selections, lesson examples, teacher questions, and class projects can all be used to allow boys and girls to freely engage in learning by questioning stereotypes of femininity and masculinity as well as follow areas of interest.

On the other side of the debate, an often-cited report looks at the negative social effects of students in single-gender classes. In 1997, California Governor Pete Wilson funded several schools that started single-gender programs. Though there were difficulties in implementation, researchers found that "Traditional gender stereotypes were often reinforced in the single-gender academies. Boys tended to be taught in a more regimented, traditional and individualistic fashion, and girls in more nurturing, cooperative and open environments" (Datnow, Hubbard, & Woodly, 2001, p. 7).

Certainly, the danger of exacerbating stereotypes is real within single-gender programs. And that is why, later in this book, the need for staff

Table 1.7 Data From New York State Report Card, 2007

					New York: Percent of Students Scoring a 1 (not meeting standard) or 2 (partially meeting standard) on State Assessment, 2006–2007																		
Gender	3rd Grade				4th Grade				5th Grade				6th Grade				7th Grade				8th Grade			
Subject	Reading		Math		Reading		Math		Reading		Math		Reading		Math		Reading		Math		Reading		Math	
Level	1	2	1	2	1	2	1	2	1	2	1	2	1	2	1	2	1	2	1	2	1	2	1	2
Female	7	29	4	14	6	28	6	20	4	30	5	24	2	33	8	28	4	37	6	31	4	37	11	39
Male	11	36	5	15	10	35	6	20	6	34	6	24	3	30	10	29	7	47	9	35	8	48	13	43

Source: New York State Report Card, 2007.

Table 1.8 Data From Illinois State Report Card, 2007

					Illinois: Percent of Students Scoring a 1 (not meeting standard) or 2 (partially meeting standard) on State Assessment, 2006–2007																		
	3rd Grade				4th Grade				5th Grade				6th Grade				7th Grade				8th Grade			
Subject	Reading		Math		Reading		Math		Reading		Math		Reading		Math		Reading		Math		Reading		Math	
Level	1	2	1	2	1	2	1	2	1	2	1	2	1	2	1	2	1	2	1	2	1	2	1	2
Female	3.6	19.0	3.1	9.7	0.5	22.5	0.8	11.9	0.5	26.0	0.4	15.9	0.1	22.8	0.3	16.5	0.3	22.2	1.7	17.8	0.3	13.6	0.9	16.2
Male	7.0	24.3	4.3	9.4	1.5	27.9	1.5	13.1	1.0	33.0	0.7	18.0	0.3	29.9	0.7	19.5	0.7	29.9	2.8	18.8	0.8	21.6	1.5	18.8

Source: Illinois State Report Card, 2007.

Table 1.9 Data From Washington State Report Card, 2007

	3rd Grade				4th Grade				5th Grade				6th Grade				7th Grade				8th Grade			
Washington: Percent of Students Scoring a 1 (not meeting standard) or 2 (partially meeting standard) on State Assessment, 2006–2007	Reading		Math		Reading		Math		Reading		Math		Reading		Math		Reading		Math		Reading		Math	
Subject / Level	1	2	1	2	1	2	1	2	1	2	1	2	1	2	1	2	1	2	1	2	1	2	1	2
Female	8.3	14.7	13.0	16.1	4.4	17.6	21.9	22.5	5.7	15.2	14.5	21.2	5.0	20.0	21.8	26.9	6.6	23.4	27.0	19.7	6.3	20.0	21.9	24.1
Male	14.4	18.7	15.3	16.4	7.7	23.1	24.5	22.0	8.9	17.2	18.3	21.7	9.3	26.0	25.6	25.6	12.0	29.2	30.1	19.6	11.5	26.2	25.1	22.0

Source: Washington State Report Card, 2007.

development before implementing a single-gender program is stressed. However, the assumption that keeping boys and girls together automatically eases stereotypes and social concerns for boys and girls is not supported by recent publications. Authors concerned with the well-being of students cite powerful data that show the vulnerabilities of each gender. Consider these statistics for girls:

- One in four girls will show signs of depression.
- One in four girls will be in an abusive relationship.
- Girls are two times more likely than boys to attempt suicide.
- Girls are five times less likely than boys to receive attention from teachers.
- By age 13, 53 percent of girls are unhappy with their body.
- By age 18, 78 percent of girls are unhappy with their body (Deak, 2002).
- Girls are three times more likely to be told to be quiet, speak softly, or talk with a "nice" voice (Simmons, 2002).

Consider these statistics for boys:

- Boys are three times more likely than girls to commit a violent crime.
- Boys are four–six times more likely than girls to commit suicide (Pollack, 1999).
- Seventy percent of special-education students are boys.
- Eighty percent of discipline referrals are boys.
- Up to 70 percent of the Ds and Fs are made by boys (Gurian & Stevens, 2005).
- One in 112 males were sentenced to prison, while one in 1,724 women were (Slocumb, 2004).

Given these statistics, one must question whether we are meeting the needs of students in a coed environment; the coed classroom would not seem to be the only model to address socialized expectations and stereotypes. Any discussion about single-gender programs involving socialization, then, should include the reality of boys' and girls' school lives.

HORMONAL DIFFERENCES

JoAnn Deak, author of *Girls Will Be Girls* (2002), writes that several hormones play an important role in the lives of girls. She explains:

> Although it is not known why, the fact is fairly well established that estrogen has an enhancing effect on some areas of the left

hemisphere of the brain, and testosterone has an enhancing effect on some areas of the right hemisphere of the brain. This means that most girls are slightly predisposed, and therefore more comfortable, with sequential, detailed, language-based factual tasks. (p. 83)

Imagine a lesson with clear beginning, middle, and end where the teacher leads students from the introduction, through modeling, to independent practice. If Deak is correct, then girls may prefer this form of learning and possibly respond better to this form of teaching. What about the boys? Perhaps they will get frustrated, be impatient with the process, or disengage from the lesson.

Deak is not the only author who puts forward the idea that hormones can influence learning. Melissa Hines (2004), psychologist and researcher on neuroendocrinology, states, "Gonadal hormones androgen and estrogen have powerful influences on the development of brain regions that show sex differences, as well as on behaviors that show sex differences" (p. 3). From this point of view, knowing how these hormones work and how they influence a boy's or girl's actions can benefit the instructional decisions of a teacher. Consider Thomas Armstrong's (2006) statement in *The Best Schools:*

Contrary to popular belief, it is not so much the direct influence of hormones on the body that is associated with the emotional turbulence of puberty. Rather, it is the impact that these hormones have on the development of the brain. Surges of testosterone at puberty, for example, swell the amygdala, an almond-shaped part of the limbic system (emotional brain) that generates feelings of fear and anger. Similarly, estrogen seems to affect serotonin levels at puberty, accounting for higher rates of depression among teenage girls. (p. 115)

No one disputes that the mix and levels of hormones in girls and boys differ. Authors vary in terms of the influence hormones have on learning. Some suggest hormones dictate everything (Brizendine, 2006). Doreen Kimura, in her book *Sex and Cognition* (1999), argues that hormones cause predictable performance differences, explaining:

Women undergo large variations in estrogen and progesterone levels across the natural menstrual cycle. Men experience changes in testosterone levels across the seasons, and within the course of the day. In both sexes, such hormonal changes are associated with predictable changes in cognitive strengths. (p. 115)

Psychologist Susan Pinker (2008) pushes the argument even further by claiming, "The level and type of hormones circulating in the bloodstream are linked with how well you solve spatial tasks, how expertly you read others' emotions, how easily you trust other people, and, not surprisingly, the types of jobs you choose" (p. 219). To some, this may sound like justification for limiting the options of students. To others, this may provide liberation to finally understand the influences within one's life and make informed choices.

Refuting the hormone argument altogether, Rosalind Barnett and Caryl Rivers, in their book *Same Difference* (2004), assert, "It seems laughable to believe that one hormone [testosterone] could be responsible for this cartoonish version of masculine behavior, and that the lack of it would disqualify one from positions of leadership" (p. 178). They say, "Blaming hormones for women's 'frailties' is an old story" (p. 183). Hines (2004), while recognizing that there are hormonal influences, cautions, "Few data are available linking structural sex differences to functional sex differences. . . . Experience can alter sex differences in brain structure" (p. 221). In the rush to provide evidence for sex differences and explanations for performance sex differences, educators and authors sometimes make an uninformed leap from the emerging science of sex differences to advising instructional practices. Only by examining different perspectives of sex differences, and reflecting on these arguments in light of one's own classroom experiences and students, can educators make informed decisions.

Clearly, hormones vary in males and females. In the context of single-gender education, the controversy centers on how much teachers should take hormonal fluctuations into account when planning lessons and interacting with students. Can the premise of hormonal differences help teachers make sense of actions within the classroom without limiting what boys and girls are capable of achieving? Should teachers consider boys' testosterone levels as an excuse for aggressive behavior? Can teachers better understand girls' interactions through the lens of the hormone estrogen?

BRAIN DIFFERENCES

Perhaps no factor of the gender issue is more hotly debated than the idea that boys and girls are born with different biological brain makeup, sometimes referred to as "hard wiring."

Leonard Sax, a family physician and psychologist, is probably the most outspoken advocate of brain-based differences between boys and girls. His book, *Why Gender Matters* (2005), is a treatise on how boys and girls are different and why these differences matter. He argues, "Stuck in a mentality that refuses to recognize innate, biologically programmed differences between girls and boys, many administrators and teachers don't fully appreciate that girls and boys enter the classroom with different needs, different abilities, and different goals" (p. 9). Sax is clearly charging educators to recognize that there are innate, biological differences in how boys and girls learn.

Brizendine (2006), from a neuropsychiatric perspective, also supports the idea there are brain-based differences between males and females. She claims:

> The female brain has tremendous unique aptitudes—outstanding verbal agility, the ability to connect deeply in friendship, a nearly psychic capacity to read faces and tone of voice for emotions and states of mind, and the ability to defuse conflict. All of this is hard-wired into the brains of women. These are the talents women are born with that many men, frankly, are not. (p. 8)

Eric Jensen and David Sousa are widely published authors on brain development and its impact on learning. They are not gender-study authors, but they have found that gender impacts student learning. For instance, Sousa, in his book *How the Brain Learns* (2006), says:

> Scientists have known for years that there are structural and developmental as well as performance differences between male and female brains. Studies begun in the early 1970s and subsequent studies by other researchers have shown some gender differences in brain characteristics and capabilities. PET scans and MRIs, for instance, indicate that males and females use different areas of their brains when accomplishing similar tasks. (p. 172)

Jensen agrees in his book *Brain-Based Learning* (2000):

> Gender issues are extremely complex. The variations within the gender groups are as great as those found between genders. This does not negate the fact, however, that in general a variety of social and biological differences between men and women exist and they impact learning. (p. 91)

There are authors who argue there are no hard-wired differences between boys and girls that are meaningful. Deborah Blum, author of *Sex on the Brain* (1997), recognizes, "Gender biology has extraordinary promise if—and this may be an insurmountable if—we are willing to give it an objective hearing" (p. 279). Later, she asserts, "We have to get away from the outdated notion that biology assigns us a fixed place" (p. 280). Lise Eliot, an associate professor of neuroscience, and Susan Bailey, executive director of the Wellesley Centers for Women (2008), announced their opinion in a *USA Today* editorial that there were no hard-wired differences between girls and boys.

Rosemary Salomone, author of *Same, Different, Equal* (2002), played a key role in revising the federal regulations that ultimately made it legal to create single-gender classes in public schools while still adhering to Title IX legislation. However, recently, she has stated, "Every time I hear of school officials selling single-sex programs to parents based on brain research, my heart sinks" (as cited in Weil, 2008, p. 41). While supportive of single-gender schools and programs, Salomone dismisses hard-wiring differences in boys and girls as an argument for single-gender classes.

A brief dip into the literature on this topic reveals diametrically opposed viewpoints, and a discussion of hard-wired differences frequently turns into a vigorous debate about which research is valid. However, often when teachers are exposed to the research-based ideas of how boys and girls learn differently, they can't help but reflect on their teaching and see their own students through that prism. Thus, they gain another framework of understanding why certain events may happen in their classroom and possibly use those observations to better meet the needs of their students.

GENDER IS AN ISSUE

How should your school address gender? This first step is to gather performance data and then reflect on stereotypes and social concerns of boys and girls in your school. Then, learn more about hormonal and brain differences debate between boys and girls. In fact, engaging in discussion about each of the four mentioned areas of gender will provide opportunities to grapple with the issue of gender and how to best educate your students. It is difficult to deny that gender plays a role in education, and whatever conclusions your school or district may reach, the issue of differential achievement needs to be faced and addressed whether in single-gender or coed settings.

Educators and parents alike will want to know what the differences are that matter for their children: What do gender differences mean within the classroom? For teachers, this is an area for professional development and is explored in Chapter 10. It is beyond the scope of this book to explore the topic of gender differences in detail, but a summary is included in Table 1.10, along with resources for further reading and ways that teachers might use the information within their classroom. The table organizes gender differences into six categories—seeing, hearing, engaging, processing, responding, and choosing—that seem to be most helpful for educators and parents. The table is not an exhaustive list, but something that can be used with parents and teachers as an introduction. Of course, caution is necessary whenever talking about gender differences, making sure that stereotypes and absolutes are not reinforced.

Table 1.10　Summary of Gender Differences

Category of Difference	Summary of Difference	Further Reading	Insight Into Classroom
Seeing	Boys' eyes tend to focus on the motion of objects and cool colors; girls' eyes tend to focus on the description of the objects and warm colors.	Baron-Cohen, S. (2003). *The Essential Difference*: pp. 76, 79 Deak, J. (2003) *Girls Will Be Girls*: p. 42 Fletcher, R. (2006). *Boy Writers*: pp. 91, 119 Hall, J. (1984). *Nonverbal Sex Differences*: p. 27 James, A. (2007). *Teaching the Male Brain*: pp. 20, 32, 39 Jensen, E. (2000). *Brain-Based Learning*: pp. 56, 95 Kimura, D. (1999). *Sex and Cognition*: pp. 91, 95 Newkirk, T. (2002). *Misreading Masculinity*: pp. 65, 170, 172, 183 Sax, L. (2005). *Why Gender Matters*: pp. 19, 20 Sousa, D. (2006). *How the Brain Learns*: p. 175	Teachers may use their own movement as an instructional tool. Teachers may focus on presentation and details of a project without emphasizing colors. Teachers may be aware of their own use of colors as well as student choices.
Hearing	Girls tend to hear better than boys and hear tones better than boys.	James, A. (2007). *Teaching the Male Brain*: pp. 19, 37, 43 Jensen, E. (2000). *Brain-Based Learning*: pp. 69, 95 Kimura, D. (1999). *Sex and Cognition*: pp. 81–82, 89 Sax, L. (2005). *Why Gender Matters*: pp. 17, 18	Teachers may be aware of their own volume and tone during instruction and question/answer. Teachers may check to see if students are being distracted by loud work time before correcting students.

(Continued)

Table 1.10 (Continued)

Category of Difference	Summary of Difference	Further Reading	Insight Into Classroom
Engaging	Boys' engagement tends to be more dominant with the sympathetic nervous system (known as the fight or flight system); girls' engagement tends to be more dominant with the parasympathetic nervous system (known as the rest and digest system).	Dart, A. et al. (2002). *Gender, Sex Hormones and Autonomic Nervous Control of the Cardiovascular System:* pp. 2–3 Jensen, E. (2000). *Brain-Based Learning:* pp. 162–163 Newkirk, T. (2002). *Misreading Masculinity:* pp. 42, 67 Sax, L. (2005). *Why Gender Matters:* p. 69	Teachers may be aware of students' need for movement and these moments as instructional opportunities. Teachers may incorporate a variety of ways for students to complete tasks and demonstrate their learning.
Processing	Girls tend to process events and information in analytical and emotional aspects, considering differing perspectives more often; boys tend to process events and information in an either/or perspective.	Deak, J. (2003). *Girls Will Be Girls:* pp. 43–44, 55–57, 197 Fletcher, R. (2006). *Boy Writers:* pp. 54, 83 Ginsberg, A., et al. (2004). *Gender in Urban Education:* pp. 78, 114 James, A. (2007). *Teaching the Male Brain:* p. 18 Jensen, E. (2000). *Brain-Based Learning:* pp. 203, 208 Jensen, E. (2006). *Enriching the Brain:* p. 102 Newkirk, T. (2002). *Misreading Masculinity:* p. 39 Sax, L. (2005). *Why Gender Matters:* pp. 29, 93 Simmons, R. (2002). *Odd Girl Out:* pp. 30–31 Sousa, D. (2006). *How the Brain Learns:* p. 173	Teachers may be aware of the overall climate of the classroom environment. Teachers may provide opportunities for students to make connections between content and applications to their own lives, and raise questions about the material.

Category of Difference	Summary of Difference	Further Reading	Insight Into Classroom
		Baron-Cohen, S. (2003). *The Essential Difference:* pp. 1, 50, 57, 66 Hines, M. (2004). *Brain Gender:* pp. 16, 17 Slocumb, P. (2004). *Hear Our Cry: Boys in Crisis:* pp. 17, 37, 64, 69, 77	
Responding	Boys tend to respond to appropriate instructional stress with alertness and action; girls tend to respond to appropriate instruction stress with anxiety more often than boys.	Baron-Cohen, S. (2003). *The Essential Difference:* pp. 30, 32, 44, 46 Maccoby, E. (1966). *Development of Sex Differences:* pp. 32–33 Rimm, S. (1999). *See Jane Win:* p. 12 Sax, L. (2005). *Why Gender Matters:* pp. 68–69, 89	Teachers may be aware of competition, time, and pace as instructional factors within the classroom.
Choosing	Girls tend to underestimate their abilities and see success as a result of hard work; boys tend to overestimate their abilities and see success as a result of being smart.	Deak, J. (2003). *Girls Will Be Girls:* pp. 223, 229 Maccoby, E. (1966). *Development of Sex Differences:* p. 32 Newkirk, T. (2002). *Misreading Masculinity:* pp. 38, 79, 94, 110, 120–121 Pollack, W. (1999). *Real Boys:* p. 8 Sax, L. (2005). *Why Gender Matters:* pp. 42–43 Simmons, R. (2002). *Odd Girl Out:* pp. 46, 84 Slocumb, P. (2004). *Hear Our Cry: Boys in Crisis:* p. 38	Teachers may be aware of the need to structure opportunities for students to develop responsibility and self-efficacy.

CHAPTER 1 PLANNING TOOL: REFLECTING ON GENDER

Use the following prompts (from the questions posed at the beginning of the chapter) to help reflect on the main ideas of the chapter and organize a plan of implementation. Agreeing with any one of these statements provides motivation to consider single-gender programs. The remainder of this book is to help those who are taking that journey.

Indicate the level of agreement you have with each statement and why. SD = Strongly Disagree, D = Disagree, SWD = Somewhat Disagree, SWA = Somewhat Agree, A = Agree, SA = Strongly Agree	
I believe students can do better than they do now. Reason:	SD—D—SWD—SWA—A—SA
I think that we, as part of the educational field, are not academically meeting the needs of our boys and/or girls. Reason:	SD—D—SWD—SWA—A—SA
I think the opposite gender negatively influences the behavior and performance of students. Reason:	SD—D—SWD—SWA—A—SA
I think teachers can better address social needs of boys and girls in single-gender classes. Reason:	SD—D—SWD—SWA—A—SA
I think hormones play an important role in how boys and girls behave. Reason:	SD—D—SWD—SWA—A—SA
I think there are hard-wired differences in students. Reason:	SD—D—SWD—SWA—A—SA

2

What We Know About Single-Gender Programs

Single-gender education may seem a very old-fashioned idea harkening back to days of primers and rows of benches in classrooms. However, single-gender education is a growing a part of the modern public school system across the country, and there are data available to help educators as they investigate this choice for their school or district.

DEMOGRAPHIC DATA

The National Association for Single-Sex Public Education estimates that there were about 400 single-gender programs or schools within the United States during the 2007–2008 school year, with the following breakdown by region:

195 schools in the Southeast

113 schools in the Midwest

51 schools in the Northeast

42 schools in the West (*Education Week,* 2008)

These data show that single-gender programs are a nationwide phenomenon. While there are definite pockets where there is an expansion of programs, there is no region where single-gender programs are not being implemented.

Looking closer, one state can provide us with important insight into the current status of single-gender education. South Carolina has been recognized as the national leader in single-gender education within the public school system (Adcox, 2007).

Why South Carolina? Timing is the answer. Four events converged to position South Carolina for the possibility of leading single-gender education in the United States. First, federal regulations were issued in 2006 making single-gender programs legal within the public school system. Second, a new State Superintendent of Education, Jim Rex, was elected on a platform of increasing public school choice—including single-gender programs. Third, one of the first single-gender public middle school programs was in its third year with very positive results, receiving positive media coverage. Fourth, South Carolina parents were accustomed to the ideas of vouchers (providing public money for private schools). Legislative bills had been introduced in the state legislature but failed for the previous three years. These four events were all in place in January 2007. Over the next several months, the dialogue about public education in South Carolina turned to providing more choices within the public schools system, changing the accountability system, and changing the way schools were funded. In July 2007, Dr. Rex created the Office of Public School Choice and hired this author to be the coordinator for a new program, Single-Gender Initiatives. The coordinator's role is to support schools as they investigate and create single-gender programs. This position was, and still is, unique in the country. Exploring the data from South Carolina and experiences in that state can be helpful in considering questions that arise about grade levels, student populations, and levels of student achievement within single-gender programs.

Grade Levels

Let's take a look at single-gender programs in South Carolina public schools from August 2007–August 2008. During that period, with the state's support, there has been substantial growth, from 82 schools implementing or considering a single-gender program to over 350 schools implementing or considering single-gender programs. Table 2.1 illustrates that growth. These numbers include public schools investigating single-gender programs and those actually implementing a single-gender program.

Table 2.1   South Carolina Schools Implementing or Investigating
Single-Gender Programs by Grade Level

Total Number SC Schools With or Investigating SG Programs	August 2007	October 2007	January 2008	April 2008	August 2008
Elementary	25	36	97	114	173
Middle	59	71	108	137	157
High	2	4	16	30	38

Source: *Gender Matters*, 2007–2008.

Often, when single-gender classes are first mentioned among educators, the tendency is to think of them within middle schools. Typically, this is because of the social difficulties that students have within middle schools, the hormonal changes that occur during these years (making gender more of an issue), and the potential difficulty students have in making the transition to a more departmentalized program. As Table 2.1 shows, in August 2007 in South Carolina, the number of middle schools with single-gender programs was more than double that of elementary schools. However, as support for such programs increased and more educators learned about single-gender classes, the number of elementary schools interested in single-gender classes surpassed middle schools, and now there are more elementary school programs within the state. The number of middle schools also increased, from 59 to 157; by August 2008, roughly 70 percent of the middle schools in the state had either implemented single-gender programs or were investigating the possibility. At the high school level, there wasn't as much awareness of single-gender options, but the number of schools exploring the idea grew from 2 to 38—a very large increase.

In South Carolina, the overall increase occurred for many reasons. Some schools are seeking ways to meet the individual needs of students; others are searching to find alternatives and choices for programs they already are offering; still others are looking for ways to revise current strategies to have a greater impact on student learning. Importantly, no matter the students' ages, it is the determination of the principal, dedication and passion of teachers, and resolve of parents that ultimately allows single-gender programs to take hold and flourish.

Student Populations

Nationally, the demographics of schools and communities with single-gender programs vary widely. There are lower elementary charter schools for inner city boys, high schools for girls in New York City, and a set of boy and girl schools serving Cleveland, Ohio. Dotted across the country, there are multiple schools that have instituted single-gender classes.

Again, using South Carolina as an example, there is a broad range within the demographics of school communities with single-gender programs. Seeing this range offers support and confirmation to others who are considering a program at their own schools.

There are single-gender programs operating within schools with a high percentage of students receiving free or reduced-price lunch and there are programs in more affluent communities. Single-gender programs are operating in schools where students are 99 percent African American or Caucasian, and in schools of many different subgroups.

Table 2.2 shows the average percent of students by subgroups within elementary, middle, and high schools in South Carolina. The range of percentages is also included.

Table 2.2   Demographic Information on South Carolina Schools With Single-Gender Programs

Showing Average Percent and Range in Parentheses			
	Elementary n = 70	*Middle* n = 94	*High* n = 19
Boys	52% (43–64)	51% (20–57)	51% (46–60)
Girls	48% (36–57)	49% (20–65)	49% (40–54)
African American	44% (0–97)	50% (0–99)	43% (0–89)
Caucasian	50% (0–100)	46% (1–100)	54% (9–100)
Other	7% (0–33)	5% (0–33)	5% (0–12)
Free/Reduced-Price Lunch	68% (13–96)	60% (0–99)	57% (11–87)

Source: *Gender Matters,* 2007–2008.

This chart illustrates the wide variety of situations in which single-gender programs operate. The information defies the idea that single-gender programs can only exist within a limited demographic student population. Single-gender programs can meet the needs of many communities and their individual students.

Despite popular misconceptions, we cannot say that there is one area where single-gender programs "work" best. Nor can we say that there are particular students who benefit more or less from single-gender programs. Single-gender programs can present a choice for parents with students at all grade levels, achievement levels, and race.

Next, let's look at the data on student achievement.

ACHIEVEMENT AND OTHER DATA

We live in a data-driven educational system. With high-stakes testing holding students, teachers, principals, and superintendents accountable, everyone wants to know what happens to student achievement within single-gender classrooms. Do single-gender programs actually work? This is the question that almost every administrator asks. It is an important question, but currently the answer is elusive. The definition of "working" can vary by school as each school implements its program for a different purpose. However, the most common understanding of a program working is its positive effect on student achievement, discipline referrals, student self-concept, dropout rate, student participation in class, student course selection, or perceived gender stereotypes.

Complications With Data Collection

Before looking at examples of concrete data for administrators and teachers to consider, it is important to understand the current challenges and limitations with data collection related to single-gender education.

1. *There are many variables at work.* Because single-gender education in public schools must be "completely voluntary," it may be impossible to isolate the single-gender program as the sole variable in a research study or reporting of data. Reading programs, math programs, or enrichment programs also exist at many schools and could be factors related to a variance in student achievement. Also, the fact that parents choose to have their child in a single-gender program makes parental choice a variable when researching single-gender programs. Some researchers argue that any success with single-gender programs is due to greater parent involvement.

As Gerald Bracey (2006), an independent researcher on single-gender programs, notes, "It is extraordinarily difficult to conduct scientifically acceptable research on single-sex schools. The mere fact that all such schools are schools of choice means that from the outset, no random assignment is possible" (p. 16). In addition, there is great variation among the programs, with how teachers were trained, and resources available to students. This issue is one that hopefully will be researched more in the near future. Currently, principals and teachers have anecdotal successes to reference while waiting for researchers to gather "hard" data.

2. *The track record is short.* The reemergence of single-gender education within public schools has occurred only recently. As a result, there simply has not been enough time for longitudinal research studies to be designed and implemented. There are some major universities currently seeking federal funding to conduct longitudinal studies in South Carolina. Doctoral and master's candidates also continue to research single-gender education for their programs. Synthesizing these data would be a benefit for all involved in single-gender education.

Importantly, individual schools are starting to gather their own data on student achievement, attendance, and discipline within single-gender programs. Most of these data do not come in the form of a controlled research study, but as isolated results or anecdotal evidence. Nonetheless, learning about the different ways that schools with single-gender programs are able to meet their own goals and to report success either by achievement, attendance, or discipline can encourage other educators to start considering and exploring single-gender education. In South Carolina, schools with single-gender programs are asked to submit an annual review of their program. A copy of the review form is in Resource E.

3. *Comparisons to coed classes aren't helpful.* Current single-gender classes should not always be compared to current coed classes with the same school. While administrators would certainly want single-gender classes to be successful in meeting program goals, school administrators encourage and support all of their classes, programs, teachers, and students to be successful. Comparing, for example, the achievement or discipline level of current single-gender classes to current coed classes can create an either/or competition that is not necessary or helpful to either single-gender or coed classes, or teachers. An alternative could be to compare the results of the students in single-gender classes with averages of students from coed classes during the years before single-gender classes were implemented at the school. Formats for program evaluation are explored in Chapter 11.

Remember, single-gender classes are not designed to overtake or necessarily outperform coed classes. Rather, the programs are a way for schools to meet the needs of individual students, and to provide a choice for parents.

As such, a single-gender class may be good for some students and not others. Comparing students from single-gender and coed classes assumes that one must do worse in order for the other to be validated, when in reality it is the growth of the student that really matters. The most significant achievement number is the comparison of student performance at the start of the school year with performance at the end. What did the student learn?

Did the program benefit the student? We can never know how well the student would have done in another environment or with another teacher.

4. *No standard data collection is required.* Interestingly, the federal regulations do not require that data be reported. Schools need to only review data that reflect their rationale for creating a program, also demonstrating that the program was not created with broad stereotypes. The type of data is not defined nor is the process under which the data are reviewed. If a school created a single-gender program in the hopes of increasing academic achievement, then student achievement numbers would be used to review the single-gender program. The type of data necessary is not defined by the federal regulations.

In addition, schools only need to review their data every two years. And again, there are no specific ways data must be reviewed. If a school started a program in the fall 2007, they would not have to collect and review their own data until summer 2009. Practically, however, district administrators, the media, and parents will more than likely request information regarding the impact of the single-gender programs, and it would be wise for principals to be able to describe the effect of the program in some substantial way.

Collection of data is important to support any new educational program. However, understanding the constraints under which research can be conducted among single-gender programs is necessary. More research clearly needs to be conducted. Principals and district administrators should strive to make the successes and weaknesses of their single-gender programs public, and be open to national research efforts to quantify the impact of public school single-gender programs.

Recent Studies on Single-Gender Programs

The most recent national studies on single gender were released in 2005 (U.S. Department of Education) and 2006 (Bracey). Both studies were meta-studies and screened hundreds of smaller studies, selected the ones that fit their criteria, and analyzed the remaining items. The studies set about to compare single-gender programs with coed programs, and failed to find a definitive benefit for either. The U.S. Department of Education 2005 study reported:

It is more common to come across studies that report no differences between SS [single-sex] and CE [coed] schooling than to find outcomes with support for the superiority of CE [coed]. In terms of outcomes that may be of most interest to the primary stakeholders (students and their parents), such as academic achievement test scores, self-concept, and long-term indicators of success, there is a degree of support for SS [single-sex] schooling. (p. xvii)

Bracy's 2006 study reported:

Of 2,221 quantitative studies, only 40 survived a review from the American Institutes for Research commissioned by the National Center for Education Statistics (NCES), even though the review had relaxed its criteria for judging studies methodologically adequate. Those included in the NCES review reported on 33 outcomes, ranging from achievement test scores to graduate school attendance to self-esteem to unemployment rates and even to duration of first marriages. The findings do not form a coherent body and therefore the single recommendation possible is that:

- A series of specific questions should be asked of any proposal for single-sex schools or classes. (pp. ii–iii)

Take a closer look at the findings of Bracey (Table 2.3).

Table 2.3   Results for the School Gender Categories With the Largest Number of Studies Variables, 2006

	Total	SS Male	SS Female	CE Male	CE Female	0 Male	0 Female
All-Subject Achievement	9	3	6	-	2	1	-
Math Achievement	14	1	-	2	-	8	12
Science Achievement	8	1	2	-	-	7	5
English Achievement	10	2	-	-	-	7	7
Self-Concept	7	2	3	-	-	4	4
Self-Esteem	6	1	-	2	-	3	3
Course Enrollment	14	1	4	1	1	9	8

SS Male: positive outcomes for boys in single-sex schools

SS Female: positive outcomes for girls in single-sex schools

CE Male: positive outcomes for boys in coeducational schools

CE Female: positive outcomes for girls in coeducational schools

0 Male: no difference for boys between single-sex and coeducational schools

0 Female: no difference for girls between single-sex and coeducational schools

Source: Bracey, 2006

While there are numerous studies that show no difference for boys or girls between single-gender and coed classes, this may simply show the variability of single gender with students. Remember this is the concern of pitting single gender against coed. Nonetheless, there are far more studies that show positive results for boys and girls in single-gender classes, particularly in the area of all-subject achievement.

In both cases, the number of studies that showed a benefit is clearly larger for single-gender programs. While this may not allow a researcher to claim consistency or significance, it can be viewed as something potentially positive for students within single-gender programs. That is, something good seems to be happening there for those students.

Stakeholder Voices

Student achievement, discipline, and attendance data are important, but, as mentioned, are difficult to gather. Also long-term studies have not been completed yet. However, looking at what students, parents, and teachers have to say about single-gender programs is a powerful way to get a sense of how well these programs have met the expectations of stakeholders. South Carolina, with the greatest number of programs, is a good source for these "soft" data. The state department of education conducted a voluntary, anonymous set of surveys of students, parents, and teachers who were involved in single-gender programs in the spring of 2008 and will continue to conduct the surveys annually. According to their report, roughly 2,200 students, 178 parents, and 181 teachers completed the surveys from 41 different elementary, middle, and high schools around the state. Some schools started with single-gender classes in August 2007 and others have had more experience (South Carolina Department of Education, 2008).

Highlights from each of the surveys are listed below. Students, parents, and teachers involved with single-gender classes indicate that being in single-gender classes positively impacts the learning process. Significantly, the levels of agreement are not drastically different between girls and boys.

Highlights From Student Surveys

- Overall, more than two-thirds of the students agree that single-gender education is a factor in improving each of the categories surveyed.
- Nearly three-quarters of the students agree that single-gender education is a factor in improving in desire to succeed (72 percent), participation (72 percent), ability to succeed (73 percent), and determination (73 percent).

- Female highest agreement is with desire to succeed (75 percent), independence (74 percent), participation (74 percent), ability to succeed (75 percent), and determination (75 percent).
- Male highest agreement is with ability to succeed (72 percent) and completing classwork (72 percent).
- African Americans had the highest level of agreement with desire to succeed (77 percent), ability to succeed (78 percent), and determination (77 percent).

Highlights From Teacher Surveys

- Overall, more than 80 percent of the teachers agree that single-gender education is a factor in improving each category.
- Teachers at all levels (elementary, middle, high) tend to agree at a percentage of 80 percent for each of the categories.

Highlights From Parent Surveys

- Overall, typically three-quarters of the parents agree that single gender is a factor in improving their child in each of the categories.
- The categories with the highest level of agreement for parents are self-esteem (80 percent), independence (79 percent), and self-confidence (78 percent).
- Parents believe that the teacher meets the needs of their children at a rate of 78 percent.
- Parents of boys consistently agree at a higher percentage than parents of girls that single-gender education is a factor in improving the categories, 75–85 percent and 65–75 percent, respectively.

This information is very informative for someone considering single-gender programs. In general, students, parents, and teachers like single-gender programs. Most importantly, students see the value of single-gender programs in their academic and social lives. Pedro Noguera (2008), in his account on race and education, suggests that schools have to learn what works with students: "Student motivation does have an impact on student achievement, and while it is essential that opportunities to learn are expanded, it is also necessary for schools, parents, and the community to find ways to motivate students who have come to see schooling and education generally as unimportant" (p. 157). Surveys like these from South Carolina point to something happening that turns the tide of student perception. Taking the pulse of parents, students, and teachers allows the educator to recognize that there is a positive attitude surrounding single-gender programs.

CHAPTER 2 PLANNING TOOL: USING DATA

Use the following prompts to help reflect on the main ideas of the chapter and clarify your thoughts on single-gender programs.

- What type of data is important for you?

- In what way do the data presented here support your efforts to start a single-gender program?
  o What concerns are raised?
  o Do any of the data contradict your perceptions of single-gender programs?

- What would you need to do in order to gather quality data?

Create a Snapshot of Your School

Use the table below to organize demographic information about your school.

	Number of Boys	Percent Boys	Number of Girls	Percent Girls
Total Students				
Scored Below Basic or Not Meeting Standard in ELA				
Scored Below Basic or Not Meeting Standard in Math				
Scored Below Basic or Not Meeting Standard in Science				
Receive Free/ Reduced-Price Lunch				
Received Discipline Referrals				
Suspended or Expelled From School				

(Continued)

(Continued)

	Number of Boys	Percent Boys	Number of Girls	Percent Girls
African American				
Caucasian				
Hispanic				
Asian American				
Other				

- How does this information impact your decision about a single-gender program?

- Are there other schools in your district with single-gender programs? Where?

- Are there other schools in your state with single-gender programs? Where?

- Are there other schools in your region with single-gender programs? Where?

3

Political Opposition to Single-Gender Education

To some, single-gender programs are about separating students; to others, it is nothing more than sex segregation. To some, single-gender programs are about working with the differences between boys and girls; to others, it is nothing more than discrimination against boys and girls. These are the lines drawn by the American Civil Liberties Union (ACLU) and National Organization for Women (NOW), two political groups that firmly oppose single-gender education in public schools.

There have been, and continue to be, many reform models or programs that enter public schools: whole language, differentiated instruction, project-based learning, and Montessori, to name a few. There are proponents and skeptics of each, as there is with single-gender programs. The difference is that for a public school to create a single-gender program, federal regulations had to be written. And, ever since these regulations authorizing single-gender public education were finalized and issued in October 2006, the ACLU and NOW have been actively working to overturn them. With their financial backing, political lobbying power, offices in every state, and lawyers, they are important and vocal groups of which to be aware. This chapter's purpose is to create awareness of the arguments presented by these two prominent political groups and allow the reader to weigh the positions of the ACLU and NOW, which are very clear: They don't want single-gender schools or classes in public education.

WRP [Women's Rights Project of the ACLU] is dedicated to ensuring that public schools do not become sex-segregated and that girls and boys receive equal educational opportunities. (American Civil Liberties Union, 2008, para. 7)

NOW opposes the segregation of girls and boys into single-sex schools or classrooms. (National Organization for Women, 2008, para. 1)

THE LEGAL CONTEXT OF SINGLE-GENDER EDUCATION

The federal regulations issued in October 2006 provide guidelines for public schools to implement single-sex programs under the umbrella of Title IX of 1972, which states:

No person in the United States shall, on the basis of sex, be excluded from participation in, be denied the benefits of, or be subjected to discrimination under any education program or activity receiving Federal financial assistance. (U.S. Department of Labor, 1972, para. 1)

Public single-gender programs and schools need to follow certain guidelines (see Chapter 6) in order to avoid discrimination against someone based on sex. The American Civil Liberties Union and the National Organization for Women, however, categorically believe that separating boys and girls is a form of segregation and that segregation by definition is harmful.

The October 2006 change was perceived as a setback by the ACLU and NOW, both of which championed the passing of Title IX. Today, both organizations are involved in a vocal editorial campaign to sway public opinion, and the ACLU has launched a legal challenge against a middle school and school district in Kentucky, as well as the United States Department of Education; at the time of publication, this case is the only legal challenge to the regulations.

DEFENDING SINGLE-SEX EDUCATION

School districts considering single-gender education need to be secure in their knowledge of these organizations' positions because their arguments—which might be shared by staff members or parents—could be repeated in local newspaper editorials, parent meetings, or school planning sessions. In addition, there may be elected officials, such as school board members, union leaders, local or state legislators, and national legislators, who favor single-gender education but cannot afford to voice support for fear of losing the support of the ACLU, NOW, and their supporters. In this section, I will respond to the main arguments made against single-gender programs, as an educator who has been involved with single-gender education—and with parents, teachers, and students in single-gender programs—since 2004.

Response #1: Single-sex education is legal.

The American Civil Liberties Union (ACLU) posts its position on its Web site as follows:

> In recent months, many school districts have introduced programs that allow for expanded use of single-sex education in public schools. Many more will introduce these programs in the coming school year. In addition to being unlawful, the rationale behind these programs is bad for kids. (American Civil Liberties Union, 2007, para. 1)

Similarly, also published on their Web site, the National Organization for Women (NOW) states:

> Although research does not show that gender is an accurate, consistent, or even useful determinant of educational needs, segregated schools and classrooms are gaining popularity. (National Organization for Women, 2008, para. 1)

Both statements point to a growth of single-gender programs, which is true. The National Association for Single-Sex Public Education claims that just four years ago, there were only a handful of public school single-sex programs, and by August 2008, there were over 400. However, the claim that single-gender education is "unlawful" is inaccurate. Public school single-gender education has been legal since the fall of 2006, when the Department of Education issued revised regulations for implementing Title IX (Federal Register, 2006). The federal regulations were issued in October and took effect November 24, 2006. Saying that single-gender education is unlawful is inaccurate and misleading.

The position of the ACLU presumes that boys and girls in separate classes will receive significantly different educations. This is not necessarily true. We teach in a day of state standards and state and national accountability. Every public school teacher in Grades 3–8 is responsible for preparing students to be assessed in terms of skills and content learned that year. Most states have a set of state standards that all teachers must teach and to which all students are held accountable. Lesson plans, pacing guides, and classroom observations are documented to ensure that teachers are teaching the necessary skills and content. To believe that boys and girls would receive different content, concepts, or skills is outdated; this is not a function of single-sex programs.

Response #2: Recent research is informative.

In the following statement, the ACLU states that the research rationale for single-gender classrooms in public schools is very weak. They assert:

> Advocates of sex-segregated schools offer pseudo-scientific work-shops to prepare public school teachers to teach sex-segregated classes. There, teachers learn about alleged brain differences between boys and girls. According to some influential advocates: When establishing authority, teachers should not smile at boys because boys are biologically programmed to read this as a sign of weakness; they should only look boys in the eyes when disciplining them; girls should not have time limits on tests or be put under stress because unlike boys, girls' brains cannot function well under these conditions; and girls don't understand mathematical theory very well except for a few days a month when their estrogen is surging. (American Civil Liberties Union, 2007, para. 2–3)

With this statement, the ACLU is questioning brain-based research through the strategies suggested by various authors. Again, this is misleading. The statement refers to "alleged" brain differences between girls and boys, but then takes issue with the instructional practices, not the actual brain differences. The two are different. Knowing their argument gives educators the opportunity to diffuse the charged language and consider evidence that other researchers have put forward. In fact, there is a growing body of resources supporting differences between the brains of females and males and how that impacts teaching and learning (James, 2007, 2009; Jensen, 2000; Sax, 2005; Sousa, 2006). While authors will vary on how much this information should be used as input for planning lessons, educators are able to discern the brain-based information from the suggested instructional practices. Educators should make sure that they review the cited sources supporting claims made by any author on gender differences, be cautious about extrapolating from science to practice and using gender differences to stereotype students. Gender differences should be used to open more opportunities for student learning, not to close them.

All authors on gender differences quickly acknowledge that there are great differences among girls and boys, and that all boys are not the same and all girls are not the same. Nonetheless, there are tendencies within genders that can help educators, and parents, understand their girls and boys and aid them in learning and becoming the best students and people they can be. As William Pollack, author of *Real Boys* and *Real Boys' Voices*, said at the National Conference for Single-Sex Public Schools in October 2008, it isn't the science that is bad, but the application. It is non-productive to continue to turn away from growing evidence and information that can be used to enlighten teaching practices and meet the needs of individual students. It is like pounding away at a wall with a sledgehammer, trying to make an opening, while someone next to you opens a door and shows you a different way that may be more effective.

Response #3: Differences are not stereotypes.

Next, the American Civil Liberties Union (ACLU) offers a socialization argument:

> Although these ideas are hyped as "new discoveries" about brain differences, they are, in fact, only dressed up versions of old stereotypes. (American Civil Liberties Union, 2007, para. 4)

The National Organization for Women states:

> NOW recognizes that so-called "separate but equal" policies rarely treat girls equally, often relying on outdated sex-stereotypes about girls' and boys' interests and abilities. Further, studies show that all-boys schools increase sexism and exacerbate feelings of superiority toward women. (National Organization for Women, 2008, para. 1)

It is true that stereotyping students can limit teachers' expectations, thus limiting student learning. However, making lessons meaningful involves finding students' interests and their learning styles, and there is a fine line between that and gender stereotypes. For example, a teacher at a South Carolina high school described his first experiences with single-gender classes, and the increased involvement of his male students in history when approached through the perspective of wars: "The questions and discussions have seen more class involvement without the worry of not being 'cool.'"

The ACLU and NOW might point to this as evidence that the teacher is perpetuating the stereotype of boys liking war. However, it is also possible that the teacher is making history more interesting for boys by starting lessons or units with something that engages their attention.

It is right that the ACLU and NOW should caution teachers to be aware of and careful not to promote stereotypes, but their refusal to examine reputable scientific studies from multiple researchers is not helpful to teachers, students, or parents. In fact, it would be helpful for such organizations as the ACLU and NOW to fund a balanced study to examine the issue of stereotyping within public school coed and single-gender classes. That effort would be worth supporting.

Response #4: Single-gender education can blend with other reforms.

Next, the American Civil Liberties Union turns to performance:

> Creating sex-segregated schools and classrooms is a waste of time and effort that diverts resources from initiatives that actually will improve the education of both boys and girls—such as reducing class sizes and increasing teacher training. (American Civil Liberties Union, 2007, para. 4)

First, it is a false argument that single-gender education necessarily requires additional major resources, as will be discussed in Chapter 9. Certainly, starting a program or school involves funds, but the single-sex aspect of a school can be effectively implemented at little cost.

Furthermore, single-gender classes are not a zero-sum initiative: They do not exclude the possibility of small class size (nor do they require it) and single-gender education can increase teacher training, dialogue, and reflection. Teachers attend workshops, conduct book studies, and engage in meaningful collaborative planning sessions, which all benefit the education of students. Chapter 10 will provide various suggestions for professional development that do not drain resources.

Response #5: Single-gender provides a choice.

The final argument of the ACLU and NOW returns to the role of schools in preparing students for adult life:

> Moreover, these sex-segregated classes deprive students of important preparation for the real, coeducational worlds of work and family. Rather than offering choice, sex-segregated programs limit the education of both boys and girls. (American Civil Liberties Union, 2007, para. 4)

> To promote workplace equality in future years, we believe collaborative interaction between girls and boys in primary and secondary schools should be fostered, not eliminated. (National Organization for Women, 2008, para. 1)

These arguments present a common and real concern from parents and educators when they first hear about single-gender programs. This is the idea that the "real" world is coed, so education should be coed.

Educators who are considering single-gender education need to grapple with this issue and determine how they will respond. When hearing about single-gender classes, people quickly imagine all-boys and all-girls boarding schools where interactions with the opposite sex are not allowed. While this is one form of single-sex education that can benefit students, it is not a public school format. Public schools are either all-boy or all-girl for the school day, are dual academies with single-sex classes for the school day, or are coed schools offering some single-sex classes within a coed day. In the latter case, girls and boys interact during recess, related arts classes, at meals, and in the halls. In all cases, teachers can create opportunities for structured interaction of boys and girls during club activities, guest speaker events, science fairs, afterschool programs, or even during presentations of content related lessons.

In addition, I would also suggest that schools are not mirrors of the real world. They are preparations for the real world: the world of citizenship, work, and relationships. The single-gender option allows boys and girls the opportunity to develop the skills necessary to meet the demands of the coeducational world. Are all boys and all girls developing the skills necessary for a coeducational world if they are more worried about what the opposite sex thinks of them during class? Why would we not give some students the chance to prepare themselves in an environment that is better suited for them?

PARTING WORDS

The American Civil Liberties Union and the National Organization for Women raise issues for all educators interested in single-gender education to consider. In fact, they serve an important role: that of ensuring educators and policymakers who question what they do. Single-sex education can provide a powerful learning choice for parents. Being committed to making this choice a reality means successfully navigating obstacles, including the questions raised by these organizations.

CHAPTER 3 PLANNING TOOL:
DEBATING SINGLE-GENDER EDUCATION

Use the following table to help reflect on the main ideas of the chapter and prepare for future conversations with people about single-gender education. Each of the five issues is listed. In the middle column, jot down your opinion about each issue, pro and con. In the last column, write down any examples or reasons that support your opinion.

Issue	Your Opinion	Examples or Reason
1. Legality of single-sex programs.	Pro/Legal:	
	Con/Illegal:	
2. Impact of brain-based research.	Pro/Useful for teachers:	
	Con/Unfounded:	
3. Influence of stereotypes.	Pro/Not strengthened in single gender:	
	Con/Strengthened in single gender:	
4. Use of resources.	Pro/Good use of resources:	
	Con/Waste of resources:	
5. Offer of choices.	Pro/Single gender offers a choice:	
	Con/Single gender removes choices:	

- How would you respond to an editorial or article attacking your proposed single-gender program with arguments similar to the ones used by the ACLU and NOW?

4

Frequently Asked Questions

I was surprised at how well it [single-gender program] is actually working. I thought it would be much more challenging.

—Seventh-grade teacher

Implementing a single-gender program is not without difficulties. Issues and concerns come from parents, students, teachers, media, and administrators. Many of these issues are briefly addressed in other places throughout this book; here they are more thoroughly addressed in this Frequently Asked Questions (FAQ) format.

QUESTIONS ABOUT SOCIALIZATION

When will students have a chance to socialize with the opposite sex?

Concern: Students at all grade levels like to interact with the opposite sex. Many elementary school boys and girls say their best friends are girls and boys, respectively. They want to have time to talk and play with them.

Middle school students also want to talk to longtime friends of the opposite sex, as well as start new friendships. If high school students can't socialize, they often feel captive.

Options: Many schools of all levels address the issue of socialization by having recess and lunch as coed time periods, particularly if they design a program where the academic periods are single gender. In addition, related arts periods tend to be coed as well, where students are able to interact with a variety of students. Because related arts teachers may feel their instructional time is less valued since it can be used as a socialization period, it is critical that all staff members understand why a single-gender program is being created, and the compromises that may be necessary to make the program a viable part of the school. Furthermore, all teachers, whether in single-gender or coed classes, should be included in training, book studies, and meetings regarding single gender. Related arts teachers teach the same students as the teachers of single-gender classes and need to know what strategies, issues, and successes are happening.

Another option for students is to stress that school is for their future and after school is for their socialization.

Other schools specifically create afterschool clubs or activities that are coed. These clubs can be academic (e.g., math club or Lego robotics) or physical (e.g., kick boxing or sports club) or hobbies (e.g., chess or book clubs). These clubs can rotate by quarter or semester in order to be flexible around student and teacher schedules. In any case, the school should organize social opportunities for students outside of the academic day.

Some schools include clubs during school time. For example, once a week, such as Thursday afternoons, teachers lead a forty-five-minute activity of their choice. Students from across a grade level or the whole school, irrespective of gender, sign up for an activity of their choice for a month or quarter. In some cases, students rotate through exploratory activities before they make choices. The activities are coed and allow for socialization but certainly can support academics. In addition, community members, mentors, or speakers can be brought in during this time.

What will happen to students when they return to a coed class after being in single-gender classes?

Concern: Parents may wonder how their child will transition back into coed classes. In many cases, this concern carries with it the idea that the coed class is harsh, and that by being in a single-gender class, students lose that edge. Furthermore, parents will be concerned their child will not be able to work well with a coed teacher after experiencing specialized instruction in a single-gender class.

Options: The best response is that having at least one year with a teacher working with your child to better meet her or his needs is better than no time at all. Unfortunately, the premise of this concern is that children suffer within schools and that teachers are not responsive to student needs. It is not unique to single-gender classes. To start, principals need to support all teachers in the school and emphasize that students receive an excellent education in any class. That said, having an opportunity to work specifically in a single-gender class could allow the teacher to better meet the needs of that child.

Returning to the survey responses of students, the majority of students in single-gender classes say their self-confidence, desire to succeed, and participation increased. That said, success breeds success and teachers can't take this away from students. Teachers build learning habits every day, and if single-gender classes develop self-confidence and motivation, then these habits will carry over to coed classrooms.

Will students in single-gender classes become gay?

Concern: Homophobia is a real issue when talking about all-boy or all-girl classes. The issue arises among parents as well as among students. Parents may resist single-gender classes directly citing this issue or will probe the issue in indirect ways. They may ask questions about "appropriateness." Parents may ask questions such as "What if he is with boys all day?" or "Will she still like boys?" This issue is an extension of the socialization concern. In addition, it stems from the perception that single-gender classes are the same as all-boy or all-girl boarding schools, where there is no contact with the opposite sex before, during, or after school.

Options: First, it is important to remind parents that your school is not an all-boy or all-girl boarding school and that there are plenty of opportunities in their child's week to get to know boys and girls. I often joke with parents that there is no circuit placed in a children's heads that zaps them if they see or think about someone of the opposite sex. In some cases, this is enough to reduce parents' fear. Second, it is possible to address the issue of being gay directly. This can be touchy as there are biological, religious, and personal beliefs that intersect. Again, I tell parents that single-gender classes are about academics, not socialization. Third, it is again important to tell parents that single-gender classes are a choice.

The real world is coed; shouldn't children be taught in coed classes?

Concern: The world is coed. Everyone needs to learn how to get along with everyone else, boy and girl. The work world involves males and females; marriages involve males and females. We simply need to learn how to deal with each other, rather than hiding from each other.

Options: Absolutely, the world is coed, and in no way would educators implement a program that is detrimental to the productivity and happiness of a student. That said, it is important to remind parents what student surveys say about single-gender programs: Many students say their self-confidence and independence increase in this setting. If students see themselves in this way, they may be in a stronger position when developing coed relationships and not necessarily fall into stereotypical roles of male and female. It is also necessary to remind parents that these are single-gender classes and not boarding schools.

Another approach to address this issue is that some students need a different environment to develop their talents, and that a coed environment may not suit them. The single-gender classroom may shelter children from issues within a coed classroom (i.e., opposite-sex pressure or teasing), but once children have developed self-confidence and academic skills, then they can be successful in a coed situation. This goes along with the idea of scaffolding for students and meeting the needs of individual students—something that we do every day in education through accommodations, modifications, inclusions, extensions, pullouts, small groups, and differentiated instruction. We no longer teach in a world where every child is perceived as the same type of learner.

In some cases, the single-gender option provides an experience for the child that is lacking at home. For some boys, an all-male class provides male bonding that might not exist in homes without fathers or brothers. One parent informed me that she was thrilled her son was in all-boys second-grade class because his father was in Iraq and she wanted her son to have a male influence. In this case, this parent sees the single-gender option as a way for her son to prepare for the coed world.

QUESTIONS ABOUT PLANNING

Why are students in single-gender classes?

Concern: Students may initially see themselves as being punished by being in a single-gender class. They may ask, "What did I do?"

Options: It is important to remember that single gender is a choice and that parents cannot be forced to keep their child in a single-gender class. However, it is necessary to explain to students, parents, and the community the reasons for creating the single-gender program and the benefits that come from it. To redirect students from seeing themselves as prisoners, emphasize to them that more windows of opportunity will open as their academic performance increases and that they will have chances to participate in ways that weren't possible before. This could turn into an opportunity for students to set goals for the week, month, quarter, and year.

What is the long-term plan for
single-gender programs in the district?

Concern: If an elementary school is considering a single-gender program, then parents will want to know what the plans are for the middle school. If a middle school adds the program, then what about high school? Parents may not want to get involved in something that will last for just one year.

Options: District personnel need to be aware of a school's plan and coordinate what is going on with single-gender programs throughout the district. While this may seem obvious, it is not generally the case. Many principals begin single-gender programs as an experiment without district approval or knowledge. Parents tend not to want their child to be a case study or guinea pig. While long-term district plans need not be created in the beginning, some statement about what could happen within the district is important. For instance, a district may say, "The district supports single gender across all of its schools, but leaves the decision with the principal at each school as single gender best fits that location." Or, "The district is moving slowly and will examine needs and successes each year, then extend the program as necessary." Or, "There are no plans to extend the single-gender program at this time." All of these statements provide parents with the assurance that the district is aware of the single-gender program and how it fits within district initiatives.

What happens if a parent wants to switch a child
out of single-gender classes in the middle of the year?

Concern: This question is the greatest concern for principals since it could potentially unravel the entire program.

Options: Principals should meet with parents to determine if the concern is related to the class being single gender or another issue, and subsequently work with parents and teachers to resolve conflicts before moving a child. However, federal regulations clearly state the placement within single-gender programs is "completely voluntary." As such, denying a request to move a child out of a single-gender class, even in the middle of the year, could be seen as a violation of the federal guidelines. At this time, the federal regulations do not specifically address the question of timeliness.

What happens if there are more parents who
want single-gender classes than the program can support?

Concern: Parents may make more requests than there are available spots in a single-gender program. For example, a school prepares for one all-boy and one all-girl class at one grade level. But not only are there more parents who request single gender for that grade level, but parents at other grade levels request single-gender classes.

Options: Planning is key. Determining the minimum and maximum number of students in a single-gender class is essential.

If a school has overwhelming positive response to single-gender classes, then the principal can create additional single-gender classes, but this could disrupt the master schedule. Nonetheless, principals should try to meet the parents' requests.

Another option is to select students to be in the single-gender classes. Most principals use a scheduling process for single-gender and coed classes that includes blending students by race, academics, special needs, and discipline concerns. Principals can first categorize students and then randomly select students for single-gender classes who opted into the program. One principal placed students into diverse single-gender classes, and then randomly selected two classes and removed the boys and girls who did not opt into single-gender classes. She then found similar students who requested single-gender classes but were placed in coed classes, and made the switch.

Selection for single-gender classes should not be on a first-come, first-served basis. Issues of fairness and access to information will undoubtedly arise. All reasonable measures to inform parents of the program should be made, whether creating an opt-in or an opt-out program.

Should a child automatically be enrolled in a single-gender program year after year, or should there be a selection process each year?

Concern: Parents who select single-gender classes during the first year will want to know if their child can remain in single-gender classes. For instance, a program starts in third grade with one class of boys and one class of girls, and each year the program adds the next grade level. The program starts with third grade, the next year it will have third and fourth, and the year after that it will have third, fourth, and fifth grades. Will the student who starts in a single-gender class in third grade have the opportunity to stay in single-gender classes in fourth and fifth grades? Or, will principals want to add students who transfer to the school or whose parents were hesitant at first? And if the program does not grow, which students will be allowed to be a part of the program?

Options: There are four options that address this concern. The first is that students in the program from the beginning are automatically enrolled in single-gender classes but given the option to opt out. If there are open spaces due to students leaving, additional students can be placed. The most common approach is for principals to inform all parents about the single-gender program and ask for opt-in statements.

The second option is to expand the program with additional single-gender classes as the need rises.

The third option is to open the selection process each year and not guarantee any placements. This option is the most fair and objective each year, although it doesn't elicit loyalty to the single-gender program.

The fourth option is to strictly follow the rationale for creating the program. The school may have designed a single-gender program for a specific type of student based on academic qualifications: high, low, or average achievement. If the number of students who qualify is over the maximum class size, they are given the option to opt out. Hence, a student who qualifies for the program one year may not qualify the next. One particular school created a single-gender program for students who scored below basic on all four areas of the annual state assessment. These students were placed in single-gender classes, and parents were given the option to opt out. The next year, these students either remained or were removed based on their scores. New students were added based on their scores. However, some parents did not want their child removed because they saw that their child was successful. The school modified the program and had initial selection in sixth grade, based on a student's performance on state assessment. These students were allowed to remain in the program for all three years. Additional students were added based on performance, if space was available.

QUESTIONS ABOUT INSTRUCTION

Will bullying increase for boys and girls?

Concern: Putting a group of boys together and a group of girls together will quickly diffuse the distractions and potential negative interactions that occur within the classroom. However, boys and girls still bully each other. Boys can try to be the dominant male in the classroom and break down class dynamics. Girls can form cliques, and "relational aggression" can surface quickly.

Options: The principal and teachers know their students and which groups or grade levels are likely to develop bullying tendencies. Bullying in any class should be dealt with proactively and immediately, and a single-gender format is no different. This issue is frequently addressed through early and frequent team-building activities among the boys and the girls. Each group can do similar team-building activities, but the dynamics and discussions often take a different path.

Two key issues seem to arise among single-gender team-building activities. For the boys, the activities should involve physical interaction where the whole group has to work together to accomplish a goal. "Mission Impossible" activities require cooperation where the whole group has to get from one location to another using selected materials and not touching the ground. Rope courses are also good team-building activities. A simple ball toss activity can also be used to develop cooperation among students. A description of this activity is included in Resource C.

For the girls, team building should involve the dynamics of friendship. "Mission Impossible" activities and ropes courses are beneficial for girls as well, since they rely on others to succeed. However, the way girls interact with each other, even in team-building activities, often has the potential for drama. As such, helping girls understand and label the dynamics that are involved in friendships is critical. Facilitating the way that girls interact during team-building activities will help girls learn how to better work together in the classroom. A sample activity is included in Resource C. Books by Rosalind Wiseman and Rachel Simmons are helpful in gathering ideas for working with girls.

If team building is not successful or feasible, then a student may need to be removed from the single-gender classes. This isn't the ideal situation, but as with traditional classes, changes in classroom environment and student dynamics are used to quell aggressive student behavior.

How will teachers be able to control the boys and their energy? How will teachers keep girls from talking all the time?

Concern: Before teachers start in a single-gender program, these two questions often arise. These questions stem from a misunderstanding of boys and girls.

Options: The answer is simple. You don't. You don't control boys, and you don't keep girls quiet. In a single-gender classroom, and hopefully more often in a coed classroom, teachers are able to work with the tendency for boys to move and for girls to talk. This is scaffolding for students. As such, teachers should think about the appropriate time and way to work movement into the lesson for boys, and work discussion into the lesson for girls. It needs to be noted that movement for boys can involve discussions (going to different corners in the room based on a response to a question and discussing their reasons) and that discussions for girls can involve movement (talking with partners across the room or role-playing a scene from the text).

Should students in single-gender classes stay in one all-boy or all-girl group through all of their classes?

Concern: This concern grows out of the socialization issue. Essentially, will students in the single-gender classes have opportunities to interact with other students, either in single-gender or coed classes, during the day? If students stay together all day, then they can learn how to work really well together, but they can also have conflicts and issues that linger from class to class.

Options: If a school has only one all-boy and one all-girl class, then it is impossible to shuffle students within single-gender classes. In this case, it is important to build in coed classes or times to increase interaction with students of the opposite sex so they don't feel isolated.

If there are two or more all-boy and all-girl classes, then there is the possibility of reshuffling students for different subjects or periods of the day, even in elementary school. For example, students can be in the same group for English language arts and social studies but then change for math and science.

Does single-gender education increase stereotypes?

Concern: This question should be in the teacher's mind each day, whether single-gender or coed, as related to gender as well as race, nationality, economic status, religion, etc. The issue is more of a concern in the area of gender. Do teachers decorate their boy classrooms with footballs and basketballs? Do teachers assume boys do not care about other's feelings? Do the teachers decorate their girl classrooms in pink, with bows and stuffed animals? Do they use shopping examples in their lessons?

Options: Looking within is the first step in being aware of stereotyping. Knowing your students is the second step. This can be done through student-interest inventories, get-to-know-you activities, and general conversations with students before and after class. Being attuned to what they talk about, write about, and choose to read helps teachers know their students. In the effort to make lessons meaningful, teachers often use examples that are familiar to students. Using statistics from baseball teams to calculate averages makes sense if the teacher is in tune with the students. Having students create their own periodic table for a collection of items that interests them (e.g., cars, musical groups, football teams, or shopping stores) can help students understand the concept being taught.

The third step is to offer choices to students. Choice is a hallmark of differentiated instruction, and using gender differences is really a form of differentiated instruction. Providing students with a choice of topics to research, products to produce, or methods to reach the endpoint keep the issue of stereotyping at bay. Recall from the South Carolina student survey that students indicated their interest in trying new things increased as a result of being in single-gender classes.

How do I decide if I should teach all boys or all girls?

Concern: Placement of teachers is important. The issue here is lesson planning and preparation. How many prep sessions will a teacher have? Ideally, a teacher will have different procedures for all-girl classes and all-boy classes, as well as coed classes. Remember, this does not mean that boys and girls are learning different concepts or skills, but the procedures, pacing, and order of instruction can be different.

Some teachers feel that teaching one gender is easier in terms of planning. Other teachers like to teach both all-girl and all-boy classes because they don't want to miss out teaching either gender.

Options: Teachers need to have input in their placement. Reflecting on questions is very helpful, such as: Which gender do you feel you teach better? Looking at your discipline referrals and test scores, what is the spread for your classes by gender? Why do you think this is the case? Which aspects of boys and girls do you enjoy? To which do you find difficult to adjust? Questions such as these will help teachers and principals ascertain who is better with girls or boys.

Of course, scheduling will be the overriding factor when determining teacher placement. Most commonly, schools set up schedules with teachers teaching boys and girls. Ideally, the teachers should not teach boys, girls, and coed classes. This is very draining on teachers and oftentimes they do not have the energy to put into planning for three different classes every day.

After teaching boys and girls for one year, many teachers ask to teach just one gender so they can focus on their strengths. When this happens, it is important that teachers coordinate their lessons and team plan to make sure that the same standards, skills, and concepts are taught.

CHAPTER 4 PLANNING TOOL: CLEARING ROADBLOCKS

Use the following prompts to clarify the issues discussed in the chapter and plan for future discussions.

- What three concerns have been addressed?
  1.
  2.
  3.

- How and when will you communicate this information to the necessary people?
  o Information to share:
  o Necessary people:
  o Method of sharing:
  o Date of sharing:

- What three concerns remain?
  1.
  2.
  3.

- How will you gather information to address these concerns?

- How important are the remaining concerns? Are they deal breakers?

PART II

Designing a Single-Gender Program

The impetus to start a single-gender program within a school or as a separate school typically comes from someone who heard about the success of such a program elsewhere, who saw a single-gender program at a different school, or who attended a session at a conference about gender differences or single-gender teaching strategies. That person could be an administrator, a parent, a teacher, or a board member. Sometimes there is an administrative mandate: "Have a single-gender program in place next year." Teachers may ask, "I have a friend who teaches in a single-gender program and loves it; can we do that?" Parents may inquire, "Have you thought about single-gender classes?" Regardless of where the spark starts, the principal typically becomes the point person or at least the one who gives the OK to proceed. In any case, once the match is lit, in order to keep it burning without having it become a wildfire, several important steps are recommended. Those steps are the subject of the next six chapters. There are a host of obstacles with single-gender education that can arise but can be avoided with foresight and planning: legal challenges, scheduling roadblocks, and communication concerns, to name a few.

> *You don't always hear girls talking every time you work.*

—Benefit of single-gender classes according to fifth-grade boy

> *Not thinking about boys while you are learning or having them call your name every two minutes.*

—Benefit of single-gender classes according to sixth-grade girl

5

Rationale and Structure

Single-gender education means more than simply putting boys and girls in different classrooms; a successful single-gender program, as with any school initiative, involves many constituencies or stakeholders, correlates with the mission of the school, meets the needs of both boys and girls, and expands their opportunities. Implementing single-gender education requires more than a couple of recommendations. It requires a plan of action.

INVOLVE KEY STAKEHOLDERS: CREATE AN EXPLORATORY GROUP

The first step—and perhaps the most important one—is to involve multiple persons early in the process. Each principal must determine the best approach to gaining parent, teacher, and district support for a new program. Some administrators design a program and then invite teachers and parents to get on board. It is good to remember that some people resist any change regardless of its value, some resist if they have not been given adequate time to reflect on the change before it is implemented, and some resist unless they were involved from the beginning. It is safe to say, though, that enthusiastic teachers and parents are among the best allies, and they are more likely to be excited about a new program if they or their representatives have been an integral part of the program's design from the start.

Usually, the most efficient and effective place to begin is with a school improvement council, an accreditation committee, or a similar group that follows a school improvement plan. For new schools this may be the planning group. This council typically includes representative school administrators, parents, teachers, and possibly community members.

Inviting selected members to a meeting to discuss the possibility of single gender to prepare for this meeting is important. To prepare for this meeting, the principal, or designee, gathers initial information on single-gender education. Information regarding what single-gender education is, how it tends to work, and why the school is considering it would be helpful; this allows the "exploratory group" to be on the same beginning point. Previewing this book would provide a framework for the discussion. In addition, a good starting point is the South Carolina Department of Education Single-Gender Initiatives Web site (www.ed.sc.gov/sgi). Resource D also lists useful Web sites related to the education of boys and girls, including gathering data.

The initial response of the exploratory group will help determine the pace at which a single-gender program can be considered. The group may be very excited and agree with the need of having a single-gender program at the school. Plans could then move forward quickly. The group could express optimistic caution, but may want to watch programs at other schools and gather data. Or, group members could resist for any reason and determine that single gender is not a match for their school.

In the first case, action can be taken quickly. The second would take a year or two of visiting schools, having follow-up discussions, reading books and articles, gathering data, and providing professional development. While the third response could certainly end the initiative for a single-gender program, that is not necessarily the case. The commitment of principals and their ability to develop relationships with the exploratory group at their schools would likely determine the ultimate outcome. However, this would take several years of preparation.

LEARN TOGETHER ABOUT SINGLE-GENDER EDUCATION

Provided that the exploratory group determines it wise to move forward, the second step involves members of the exploratory group getting educated on single-gender education. This can include information on research-based gender differences and the potential impact within their classroom, legal considerations, and other possible programs to address needs at the school. This process could occur through book studies, visiting other single-gender classes, or attending conferences on single-gender education. The exploratory group may not agree with the idea of gender differences, but they certainly should become informed, and should weigh the information and how the information can benefit their students, if at all. Simply because there is controversy should not be grounds for ignoring the information.

ALIGN THE PROGRAM WITH THE SCHOOL'S MISSION STATEMENT

Let's assume the exploratory group is committed to moving forward and is knowledgeable about single-gender education. The next step is to ensure that the new single-gender program is appropriately aligned with the school's mission. The program or school should be integrated with the mission statement, not as an appendix.

Examining the mission statement will assist the exploratory group in presenting single-gender education as a natural extension of the school's work. Mission statements that express the desire to "create learning opportunities," "prepare for the twenty-first century," or "learn in a safe environment" may all find single gender as a natural fit. Taking the time to discuss and write down how single-gender education can blend with the school's mission can strengthen the group's resolve to implement a program and will create a more persuasive presentation to parents, school board members, and faculty members.

Even if a single-gender program fits the mission of a school, it is critical to inventory the ongoing district and school initiatives that teachers will likely be required to implement during the upcoming year. Overloading teachers with multiple initiatives can be counterproductive. Will the teachers have the time to learn about gender differences; visit other classes; and talk with colleagues about strategies, successes, and difficulties related to single gender? Single-gender education need not require new lesson plans, new teachers, new classrooms, or even new materials, but it does require time for teachers to talk, read, plan, and prepare. The school administrator should determine a timeline for implementation of all initiatives. Teachers' time needs to be respected in order for them to thoroughly embrace and implement any new or ongoing program, single gender or otherwise.

An elementary and middle school in the same district were interested in formally starting a single-gender program. In fact, these schools were physically located side by side. Each school had scheduled some single-gender classes with individual teachers and received very positive responses from teachers and students. An afternoon of professional development had been provided for the staff and the idea of single-gender education was presented to the parents that evening. The parent presentation was successful, until one parent commented that she believed in the idea of single-gender education, "but these teachers already leave the school burdened and exhausted every day. I can't ask them to do more than they are already doing."

At a different parent meeting, a parent expressed frustration that the district was starting a new way of reporting student performance without grades, was also considering uniforms, and was now looking into single-gender education. She asked, "How many things can the district start and do well and how do you expect us to keep up with these new efforts?"

DEVELOP A RATIONALE: LOOK AT SCHOOL DATA

The fourth step begins the actual design of the program: articulating a clear rationale. Not only do the federal regulations of 2006 require that any single-gender program have an educational rationale, but this step is key to giving the program substance and avoiding the perception that this educational program is simply jumping on a bandwagon or following the latest educational fad. In addition, it is likely that without a meaningful rationale, the program may not last, may meet with resistance from parents, and may be poorly implemented by teachers due to lack of clarity and purpose.

The rationale can be written by the exploratory group or other key stakeholders from the school community. Awareness of previous work is recommended so that there is consistency from the beginning to this point.

Begin by looking at data about student performance, discipline referrals, or other areas of concern for the school. Beginning with data provides an objective snapshot of the school and grounds the rationale. The federal regulations require that the rationale be written in terms of an important educational objective without overly broad stereotypes. For instance, the rationale might involve providing greater diversity of choice for parents. Data will help identify areas of need and support the articulation of objectives. For example, a school in Maine noted that statewide, boys were struggling compared to girls, with approximately 38 percent of the bachelor's degrees awarded to men by Maine's public universities (Wack, Quimby, & Menendez, 2006). In Chicago, seeing boys behind girls academically and also disciplined more often, more movement was encouraged throughout the school day by allowing children to sit on the floor or in bean-bag chairs during reading and writing activities (Banchero, 2006).

Groups can begin the process with brainstorming, interviews of parents and students, or surveys of parents and students. But at some point, sifting through the data provides a clear picture of needs. Student performance data can include standardized test scores or class grades. Data should be broken into different categories, such as performance levels or different quartiles. All data should also be broken down into specific subgroups, including gender, ethnicity, and socioeconomic status. Other information may include student surveys about school satisfaction and classroom participation.

Justification for Single-Gender Programs

1. Single gender provides greater diversity of choice for parents.

2. Single gender meets an important governmental objective.

Single-gender charter schools need not provide justification for their single-gender status in terms of the federal regulations. State charter school laws also apply, though.

While looking at the data, important questions arise: What do the data say? What observations can we make? What are the implications of the data? Are there subject areas where performance is not as expected for any specific group or overall? Is discipline at a level that is acceptable or unacceptable by any specific group or overall? Essentially, what do the data say about the students at the school?

Peg Tyre, former senior writer of *Newsweek* and author of *Trouble With Boys*, explains the process one district went through as they analyzed data:

> They [members of the school committee] looked at four years' worth of records and summarized the grades, class rank, standardized test scores, and behavioral issues for boy and girl students from second to twelfth grade. They figured out how much homework girls were doing compared to boys. They conducted careful polls to elicit feedback on how much students actually liked school, whether they felt encouraged, and how frequently they engaged with teachers. (Tyre, 2008, p. 19)

Identified areas of concern become the cornerstone for a school's rationale, which will typically address any or all of three educational objectives: (1) to increase academic performance, (2) to decrease discipline referrals, and (3) to strengthen students' socioemotional traits. By developing a rationale, a school can also determine which group of students would be best served by a single-gender program or the ideal grade level or subject area in which to offer single-gender classes. For example, if sixth-grade girls are not performing well in science while boys are struggling in language arts classes, a rationale for creating a single-gender program could be to increase achievement for girls in science and for boys in language arts. Another school may find that the first-grade reading achievement is below district or state averages. A high school may note that their dropout rate exceeds the district, state, or national averages or is simply too high. Or, a principal may note that there are too many discipline referrals in second grade, resulting in excessive student removal from the classroom and loss of time on task.

The data support the rationale and pinpoint the classes and grade levels that would benefit the most from single-gender classes. And, recall that the rationale should support and extend the overall mission of the school. When asked by parents, the media, or teachers why the school is considering single-gender education, each stakeholder should be able to draw clear parallels between the mission of the school and the rationale of the single-gender program.

Be cautious about skipping the step of creating a rationale. Not only is it required by the 2006 federal regulations, but without a strong rationale, a single-gender program is more likely to fail, due to lack of buy-in and commitment on the part of teachers and community members.

DECIDE ON A STRUCTURE

A clearly defined rationale will help schools determine which single-gender structure is best for them. No one program fits all site situations. Each school represents a unique blend of teachers, students, and has unique data that determine their rationale. Schools should consider all program structures. Each structure can be used at every grade level.

Overall, the determination of a structure should come from the rationale and can be guided by four central questions:

1. Will the program be for the whole school or focus on specific grade levels?

2. Will the program focus on all content area, the core academic time, or on specific content areas?

3. Are there enough staff members to support the ideal implementation of the program? If there are not enough, can the program start on a smaller scale? If there are more, can the program be expanded (provided there is a rationale for expanding)?

4. Can the master schedule support inclusion of the single-gender program providing for a coed option as well?

The answer to each question will guide the determination of the structure. Next, seven different structures are described, from the broadest implementation across a school to the narrowest.

1. Whole School

All classes are single gender, including core academic classes, related arts, or cocurricular courses. Lunch and recess may be single gender, as well. It is not unusual in middle school or high school that some courses may not have enough of one gender to make or fill a course and, therefore, that class would need to be coed.

Option A

Many charter schools in several states are all boys or all girls. Frequently, this is done to address a local need for some of the lowest performing students in inner cities. State laws governing charter schools need to be consulted to ensure that creating single-sex schools is allowed. For example, in Delaware, the legislature had to pass a law to allow Prestige Academy for Boys to open in August 2008 (Kepner, 2008). In either charter or traditional public schools, the school is designated as an all-boys or an all-girls school. All classes are entirely single gender. In this case, the district would need to ensure that both boys and girls have access to a substantially equal education since there will be two different locations. This option could also be considered if the district creates a magnet school that is single gender. Most likely, students from across the district would apply to attend the magnet school.

Option B

The school has boys and girls, but all classes are single gender. This is called a dual academy. Students attend all single-gender classes, including electives. Teachers teach only boys or only girls. There could be separate halls for boys and girls, each with all grade levels and subject areas (except perhaps for related arts). This would require reorganization of teacher location. At middle schools and high schools, boys and girls would probably not interact during class change. For example, during winter break in 2006, a traditional middle school in South Carolina converted core academic classes into single-gender classes. The following year, core classes continued to be single gender across sixth–eighth grades. The next year (2008–2009), the school became a single-gender academy of math and science with one wing designated for boys and the other for girls. (The coed choice was another middle school within one mile.) Students remained in their gender wing for all classes.

Option C

The school has boys and girls, and all classes are single gender as with Option B. In this option, teachers teach boys and girls, alternating classes. Teachers would probably stay in their same location. Boys and girls would likely interact during class change. This is possible for schools where students travel to different classes, usually beginning at the upper elementary level.

2. School Within a School

The majority of the classes are single gender in a separate, mostly self-contained program, and facilities are shared with the larger school. For lower elementary schools, the majority of the day would be spent in a single-gender environment. As a school within a school, this program may follow a different schedule than the larger school. In addition, there may be some different elective classes due to the program. For example, leadership academies that operate as school within a school may require a leadership course for students, or arts programs may require different arts electives.

Option A

Students apply and are selected for a magnet program. The program has specific requirements for entry and a specific mission. Teachers only teach students within the magnet program. All core classes are single gender and many related arts or cocurricular classes are also single gender. For example, a middle school magnet program was created with single gender as its cornerstone. With this, an application form, rubric, and process were also created. Information was then distributed to all of the district elementary schools, and parent nights were held to inform parents about the option. Subsequently, applications were received and processed, and admittance letters were distributed along with commitment letters for parents to sign and return, confirming that the student would attend the magnet program. All of the single-gender classes for Grades 6–8 were located in one hall of the school, even though the rest of the school was divided by grade levels (i.e., a hall for sixth grade, a hall for seventh, and a hall for eighth).

Option B

A different magnet program or specialized program is the main focus (gifted/talented, advancement via individual determination, leadership, science/math, arts), but single-gender classes are incorporated for key classes in order to maximize the effectiveness of the class, the classroom atmosphere, and the learning of the students. For example, another school district in South Carolina created a sports and fitness magnet program (for boys and girls) and the health, science, and social studies courses were designated as single-gender classes. The magnet program was not created as a single-gender program, but as a fitness program with some single-gender components that the district felt would enhance the program. Of course, there would need to be a rationale for why these courses need to be designated as single-gender classes.

3. Grade Level

A specific grade level or grade levels are single gender. All teachers of that grade level would teach single-gender classes. In upper elementary, middle, or high school, teachers could teach boys and girls or just one gender, depending on scheduling needs and staffing resources. In many schools, the program begins at one grade level and progressively builds across the school as warranted by data and parent interest. The program could start with a grade level where there is transition (e.g., from lower elementary to upper elementary, from elementary to middle, or from middle to high). For example, one elementary school successfully started a single-gender program in kindergarten, first, and second grades with the intention of adding one grade per year. At each grade level, there was a class of boys and a class of girls, as well as coed classes. The other option is to begin the program at the upper grade level and move downwards. The upper grades may be more mature and serve as leaders for the school and for the single-gender program.

Still another option is to designate one grade level as the single-gender one where there is a need for single-gender classes. For example, based upon four years of standardized test scores, one middle school found that seventh grade performance was flat and instituted single-gender classes. Similarly, a high school designed a single-gender program to address ninth-grade reading levels. An elementary school instituted single-gender classes in third grade as that was the first year of standardized test scores and students were not faring well.

4. Subject Area

Specific subject area(s) are selected for single-gender classes. Teachers in these subject areas would teach single-gender classes to boys, girls, or both. Boys and girls would mix during classes that are not single-gender. Typically, this format is used within departmentalized schools. For example, a middle school designated its math and science courses as single gender. Another middle school changed its reading enrichment program (thirty minutes of focused reading instruction to groups of students based on reading comprehension scores) to a single-gender format in order to meet the needs of the students better. Yet another middle school created its weekly advisory program within single-gender classes. Elementary schools may not be able to have designated subject areas in the single-gender format due to the fact that they are self-contained and not departmentalized.

5. Team(s)

A team of teachers teaches the single-gender classes. They are responsible for all core areas provided that there are enough students (e.g., Algebra 1 may not have enough boys or girls to make a class and needs to be coed. However, every effort should be made to fill all classes for the team in order to meet all the student's needs on the team). The team could be a pilot program and single-gender classes could expand to another format the following year or it could remain within this team. The teachers on the team may be able to teach just boys or girls, but then may need to teach two subject areas or two grade levels. Or, teachers could teach boys and girls. The different options here have to do with the selection of the students who will participate in the single-gender team. Scheduling issues are addressed in the next chapter.

Option A

Students are randomly assigned to the team. Ensuring that parents are provided with the choice to opt out is critical.

Option B

Students are selected by the faculty and the school works with parents to explain the program and reason for their child's placement within the program. Reasons could include discipline referrals (high or low), academic performance (high or low), or being on the edge of a standardized test score level.

Option C

Students apply to be a part of the team. A selection criteria, as objective as possible, or random selection procedure should be advertised to all students and used for placement.

6. Individual Teacher(s)

The rationale for a single-gender program is in place but there is only one teacher who is passionate about single-gender education (or a handful of teachers). In this case, the individual teacher would have one or more single-gender class(es) depending on scheduling constraints. This teacher believes in single-gender education and wants to make it happen. Scheduling could be particularly difficult since there may be less flexibility in times when courses are offered. In the elementary school, the teacher may be the only one in the school with a single-gender class of all boys or all girls, and this would need to be supported by the rationale. Or, there would be two teachers in the same grade level who would offer a boys' class and a girls' class, respectively. For example, two teachers in an elementary school became very excited about the possibilities of a single-gender education and wanted to switch their second-grade classes to a single-gender format. With support from the principal and district, they held a parent meeting to explain their intentions and process. One teacher would teach the boys in the morning and girls in the afternoon and vice versa for the other teacher. Parents were enthusiastic and the changed occurred in January 2008. In middle and high schools, the teacher may end up with a class of boys, a class of girls, and several coed classes.

7. Specialized Area

In this situation, single-gender classes or environments are provided within a specialized part of the school day. In each of the options, timing is important. If the events occur at the same time, then different locations with supervision need to be determined. If the events occur at different times, then a schedule needs to be established and coordinated with all other events. All of these options would need to be supported by a rationale that includes providing greater diversity of options or meeting an educational objective. Typically, the educational objective for these options involves decreasing discipline referrals, which would theoretically have an increase in student academic performance.

Option A

Breakfast is single gender. Students go to breakfast class by class.

Option B

Lunch is single gender. There is a rotation between groups of boys in the cafeteria and groups of girls.

Option C

Recess is single gender. Again, there is a rotation of boys and girls.

Option D

Classes for over-aged students are single gender. Some schools have programs designed for students who are over-aged for their grade level; in many cases the student has failed one or more previous years. These students attend single-gender classes.

Option E

The afterschool program is single gender. Classes offered after school are single gender. It is important not to stereotype student offerings and be sure that the same opportunities are available for boys and girls.

Option F

In-school detention or suspension is single gender. In this case, there would need to be two different locations and two different teachers, one for the boys and one for the girls.

CHAPTER 5 PLANNING TOOL:
DEVELOPING RATIONALE AND STRUCTURE

Use the following prompts to help reflect on the main ideas of the chapter and organize a plan of implementation.

- List possible members of the exploratory group and their role with or connection to the school.
  - o Administrators:
  - o Teachers:
  - o Staff:
  - o Parents:
  - o Students:
  - o District office members:
  - o Community members:

- Brainstorm the information to include as a single-gender introduction for the exploratory group.
  - o News articles:
  - o Brief history of single-gender education:
  - o Data from single-gender programs:
  - o Important texts:
  - o Important Web sites:

- Use the table below to organize specific data about the females and males at your school. Expand the table as necessary to include all necessary subject areas and grade levels.

	Females	Males
Academic Performance (Subject Area & Grade Level)		
Discipline Referrals (Total or Grade Level)		
Attendance Rate (Total or Grade Level)		

- Which data support the creation of a single-gender program?

  In what way?

- At this point, what are some possible rationales for creating a single-gender program?

- What are the key terms from your school's mission statement?

- Write a draft of your single-gender rationale including key terms from your mission statement.

- What are some unlikely structures for your single-gender program?

  Why?

- What are some likely structures for your single-gender program?

  Why?

- At this point, what is the best structural option for your single-gender program?

  What are the reasons?

6

Legal Issues and Logistics

"Inherent differences" between men and women, we have come to appreciate, remain cause for celebration, but not for denigration of the members of either sex or for artificial constraints on an individual's opportunity.

—Majority opinion in *United States v. Virginia et al.* (1996)
while striking down public school single-gender education

In 1996, the United States Supreme Court struck down public school single-gender education as it was being implemented at the Virginia Military Institute (VMI), under the equal protection clause of the Fourteenth Amendment of the United States Constitution (*United States v. Virginia et al.*, 1996). In so doing, the Supreme Court provided ways in which equality between the sexes could be assured. Single-gender programs remained a part of private schools and public school programs existed for several years. In 2002, with the passage of No Child Left Behind legislation, public school single-gender education was included as a permissible innovative practice. The task fell to the United States Department of Education to determine how to make public school single-gender education legal in light of the VMI case and constitutional law. The regulations were issued in October 2006 and took effect in November 2006. Public schools can implement single-gender programs (classes and schools) within the United States under federal regulations that ease restrictions for implementing Title IX (Federal Register, 2006). The United States Supreme Court has not yet had the opportunity to rule on the constitutionality of the federal regulations.

The purpose of this chapter is to familiarize administrators with the 2006 federal regulations and provide suggestions for meeting them when designing their program. The information herein does not constitute legal advice. Administrators should seek counsel from their own attorneys about the legal status of their program. First, we'll look at what the regulations require in regard to single-gender classes and programs, then at the requirements with regard to single-sex schools.

MEETING THE FEDERAL REGULATIONS FOR SINGLE-GENDER PROGRAMS

As stated in 2006, the federal regulations for public school nonvocational K–12 single-gender classes and activities include the following requirements:

1. The program must have an "important educational objective."

2. The program must be "completely voluntary."

3. The program must be "substantially equal" for boys and girls within single gender and as compared between single gender and coed classes.

4. The program can be for boys only or for girls only, or for boys and girls.

5. The program must have a coed option available.

6. The program must be reviewed every two years to determine if it is nondiscriminatory and addresses their educational rationale. (Federal Register, 2006)

Administrators and district officials need to be familiar with these regulations prior to beginning a single-gender program. The federal regulations can be accessed at the following Web site: http://www.ed.gov/news/fedregister/index.html.

Many principals may decide to begin a single-gender program as if they were implementing any other educational program. The difference, though, between a single-gender program and a program such as everyday math, reading across the curriculum, or integrated thematic instruction is that single gender has legal requirements that the others do not. In the case of public school single-gender education, not meeting federal regulations could result in a lawsuit against the school and district.

1. An Educational Objective

[T]he purpose of the class or extracurricular activity is achievement of an important governmental or educational objective, and the single-sex nature of the class or extracurricular activity is substantially related to achievement of that objective. (Federal Register, 2006, p. 62530)

Chapter 5 discussed creating an educational rationale. A single-gender program should not be implemented just because other schools are starting programs. In line with federal regulations, a rationale must be created stating educational or governmental objectives. According to the regulations, these objectives must "provide a diversity of educational options to parents and students and to meet the particular, identified educational needs of students" (Federal Register, 2006, p. 62530). As such, school leadership teams or exploratory groups looking at single-gender education need to review their own school data on achievement, satisfaction, discipline, etc. and determine what student needs exist. Of course, if there are no data to support creating a single-gender program, then one should not be implemented. In addition to the need for data to support the creation of a single-gender program, classes cannot be based upon or "rely on overly broad generalizations about the different talents or capacities of either sex" (Federal Register, 2006, p. 62531).

2. Completely Voluntary

Participation in single-sex classes and extracurricular activities must be completely voluntary . . . that recipients did not assign students involuntarily to single-sex classes. (Federal Register, 2006, p. 62531)

Making the program voluntary is potentially the most difficult part for schools, and it is the step where schools can quickly be caught in violation of the federal regulations. Suppose administrators spend time and energy creating a single-gender program only to have few parents enroll their children. Administrators might then consider putting all their students in single-gender classes, which raises several dilemmas. Would that be legal if single-gender classes are supposed to be voluntary? Should the school ask parents if they want to have their children in the program? If not enough parents request the program, should it be canceled? These types of questions arise with any new program in a school and when creating a charter or magnet school. But with single-gender classes, these questions have legal as well as instructional ramifications.

There are several ways to make a program voluntary. Overall, it is advisable to give parents the choice to opt out of the program, and it is important for the school leadership team and district administrators to agree on how a single-gender program will remain voluntary. In some cases, the design of the program will determine the selection of the students. For instance, if all of the sixth-grade core classes will be single gender, then all students will be scheduled into single-gender classes. But how do you make sure this is voluntary? Here are several options.

Option 1. Place all students in selected
single-gender classes, but parents can opt out.

Many leadership teams decide to make an entire grade level or subject area single gender due to scheduling constraints. But, placing students in a single-gender program without parental consent violates the federal regulation of making the program "completely voluntary," regardless of the intentions of the administration.

The key to making this option successful is in how the program is presented to the parents. When placing all students in single-gender classes, it is critical that parents are involved early in the planning process and in discussions about why single-gender classes are being considered. This way, parents come to understand how the single-gender classes will benefit the school and students.

Typically, the process begins with involvement of the parent-teacher organization or school improvement council. Following the decision to start a single-gender program, informational letters should be sent to parents, and parent meetings should be held often and early to inform parents about the program and gender differences. It is also wise to inform incoming students about the program so their preconceived ideas about being with all boys or all girls do not overly influence a parent's decision. The program should also reflect the overall goals for the school and not be presented as radically new. During this process, administrators and teachers will field multiple questions. If there is too much resistance to the program, then the leadership team should reconsider the design of the program and select a different single-gender structure.

Once the program has been approved, principals should send a letter to parents officially announcing the single-gender program and inviting parents to talk with them if they do not want their child to participate in the program. Principals are critical to the success of the program. Their relationship and trust with parents will carry the program.

If a parent contacts the principal about the single-gender classes, the principal will need to explain how the program operates. For a resistant parent, the principal may also want to suggest the parent give the child one month to try it, but not require it, as this violates the federal regulations. After that first month, the parent should talk with the principal again.

In most cases, the parent is concerned about change or has a misunderstanding about single-gender classes being for students with special needs, behavior problems, or remedial needs. Having parents and students try single-gender classes for a month usually is enough to have them realize the benefits of the program. However, if a parent insists on a coed option, then one must be provided in the same classes that are offered in single gender.

How is all of this voluntary? The courts, at this time, have not had an opportunity to rule on the criteria of "completely voluntary." As such, administrators are doing their best to interpret "completely voluntary" and are using reasonableness as their standard. Thus far, in the case of assigning students to single-gender classes, since parents are informed and allowed to opt out, then the program is voluntary. Essentially, if parents have been given the option to opt out and choose not to opt out of a single-gender program, then they have opted to stay in. It is their choice. Educators need to ensure reasonable efforts were made to inform parents they can opt out. This process should be done in writing: school newsletters, formal letters sent home, email correspondence, parent meetings, and newspaper announcements. However, remember that school personnel should not tell parents or students that the single-gender classes are their *only* option, which is a clear violation of the federal regulations of "completely voluntary."

Option 2. Advertise to the parent community, have parents apply, and use selection criteria to determine who will be admitted.

An alternative to placing students in a single-gender class is to inform the community about the single-gender program and invite applications. In this case, applicants are selected based upon predetermined criteria. As before, the principal should host several information nights for parents so they are familiar with single-gender education, the rationale for the program, the selection process, and how this will translate to the classroom.

With this selection process, the administration designs a program with a specific student in mind. The rationale for the single-gender program would identify the target population. The administration sets the criteria, which can be based on standardized test scores (e.g., high, low, on the edge), discipline records (e.g., none, only one, less than three), teacher and guidance referrals (e.g., student is shy, student is not meeting potential, student is bullied, student is class leader), student performance in class (e.g., A student, B or C student, D or F student), attendance (e.g., no days absent, few, many), or interviews (e.g., wants a single-gender program, is outgoing, is shy, parents are making him or her). Special education and socioeconomic status should not be used as qualifiers, since that would constitute discrimination.

With this selection process, there tends to be a correlation between rationale, program design, and the selection process. The administration should make sure that the criteria for selection is transparent to parents and made available early in the process. When determining the criteria, parents may ask questions regarding the selection process, such as: How many criteria do you have? What is the range of options? What is each criterion worth? (They do not have to be equal.) For example, if grades are considered as part of the selection process, then a rubric may be as follows: Grades (25 points) A = 25, A/B = 20, B = 15, B/C = 12, C = 10, C/D = 8, D = 5, D/F = 2, F = 0. In this case, the single-gender program targets higher-achieving students. If the rubric were reversed, then the single-gender program would target low-achieving students.

Any application process can be time consuming, but that is not unique to single gender. Once applications are received, data need to be gathered for each student and converted into points based on the rubric. Typically, students would be ranked based upon total points and a determined cut-off score. The students above the cut-off point are admitted into the program up to the class size limit, and the ones below are placed on a waiting list. Letters of acceptance or regret are sent to parents. The letters of acceptance should include a letter of commitment that the parent and student sign and return. This letter of commitment can include essential information or regulations about the program, such as honor code, dress code, or academic code. It can also include selection of cocurricular classes if appropriate. Upon receiving the letter of commitment, scheduling begins.

Option 3. Provide information to the parent community,
have them sign up, and schedule as many interested students as possible.

Providing information to the parent community and asking for interested students is the most open option for making a program voluntary. Parents receive information via newsletters, parent nights, and announcements. Letters of interest are made available through the school system or distributed to all potential students. A deadline for submitting an interest form is established.

Students should not be scheduled until the deadline passes so that placement is not based on a first-come, first-served basis. It is possible there will not be enough interest to create a single-gender program. At this point, there are two options. One, the single-gender program is postponed until enough interest can be generated. Additional information sessions, book studies, and data collection may be necessary. Two, the administration solicits parent commitment via personal communication and telephone calls.

Option 4. Target a specific group of students or individual students.

Targeting a group of students is similar to requiring an application. A criterion is determined for the students ideally suited for the program, based on the school's single-gender program rationale. However, instead of inviting parents to apply, the administration announces the program and selects students, and then solicits parent agreement. Again, the way in which this program is presented to parents is critical. It should be clearly communicated that the school is acting in the best interest of the students. In many cases, individual conferences may be necessary.

One middle school designed a single-gender program for students who scored below basic on all four subject area tests (English language arts, math, science, and social studies) in the South Carolina state assessment. Those students who qualified were placed in single-gender classes. In most cases, these classes were slightly smaller than traditional classes. Parents were notified about the single-gender program, its purpose, and the opportunity to opt out of the program.

Option 5. Randomly select students for the single-gender program.

The final option for selecting students is by designating a desired number of students for the single-gender classes and randomly selecting the students. This can be done, for instance, by using a computer program, picking names out of a hat, or scheduling every fifth student on a list. After names are selected, changes might be necessary in order to keep the single-gender classes and coed classes balanced with socioeconomic status, race, and performance level.

With all of the selection processes, it is important to communicate with parents that their child has been or has not been selected for the single-gender program.

Random selection of students can be one of the more difficult processes because parents who want to have their child in the single-gender program may not be able to participate, and parents who don't want their child to participate in the program will want their child removed. And, by federal regulations, if a parent makes such a request, the child will have to be removed. In both cases, changes will modify the list based on parent requests, which could turn the random selection process into a different process entirely.

These five selection processes are all ways in which a single-gender program can be "completely voluntary." Of course, once a court rules on the specifics of "completely voluntary," the legality of these options could change.

A middle school in South Carolina started a single-gender program in August 2008. All of its language arts and math classes are single gender. Parents were informed about the program through newsletters, parent meetings, and articles in the local newspaper.

Within the first month, a parent requested a coed option. The coed option was located at a school fifteen miles away. The parent requested a coed option be provided at the school. At first, the superintendent canceled the single-gender program. A letter was sent to parents, and appeared in the local newspaper, explaining the situation. The outcry from parents who supported the program was overwhelming. Parents were surveyed as to which program they wanted for their child: single-gender or coed. One-third of the parents requested a coed option. The school then revised its master schedule, creating appropriate coed classes and keeping as many single-gender classes as possible. Student schedules were switched at the end of the first quarter.

3. Substantially Equal

> *[The school or district] must always provide a substantially equal coeducational class or extracurricular activity in the same subject or activity. (Federal Register, 2006, p. 62530)*

This issue of "substantially equal" involves access for boys and girls to the educational process. Girls and boys need to have equal access to learning in terms of technology, textbooks, and classroom materials (i.e., science lab materials, classroom libraries, and instructional tools). "Substantially equal" also applies to, but is not limited to, the qualifications of the teachers as well as speakers, field studies, and course options.

I have had conversations with teachers and parents about how "substantially equal" may also involve the instructional activities that a teacher uses, particularly in regards to stereotyping the interests of boys and girls. For instance, an all-boys teacher may take the students to the playground for a competitive review game, whereas a teacher with girls may use cooperative groups to review the lesson. If these different methods are continually used by teachers because they believe girls learn better in cooperative groups and boys in competitive groups, this could constitute stereotyping and be substantially unequal. Other examples that could be interpreted as substantially unequal include the exclusive or majority use of hands-on materials or incorporating movement into lessons for boys, or emphasizing learning through writing more with girls. Additionally, using a variety of teaching methods only improves student learning.

The issue of "substantially equal" does not vanish once the program begins. In order to be proactive, teachers need to continually plan together in terms of pacing and instructional strategies. Certainly, teachers do not need to use identical teaching strategies, but they need to make sure they incorporate similar types of learning experiences over the duration of a unit or course. Instructional procedures should be documented within a teacher's lesson plan for review by administrators and for reflection purposes by the teacher.

4. Boys, Girls, or Both

> *[The school] must treat male and female students in an evenhanded manner in implementing its objective. (Federal Register, 2006, p. 62530)*

According to the federal regulations, a public nonvocational K–12 school can create a single-gender program for boys only, for girls only, or for boys and girls. Administrators and leadership teams need to examine the same data and the rationale for establishing a single-gender program in an "evenhanded manner" so that there is no discrimination against boys or girls. Without this step, there would be no basis for the selection of an all-boy or all-girl program.

Access to information regarding the program and opportunities available to both boys and girls must also be done in a nondiscriminatory and evenhanded manner.

5. Coed Option

> [The school or district] must always provide a substantially equal coeducational class or extracurricular activity in the same subject or activity. (Federal Register, 2006, p. 62530)
>
> Unless a recipient [school] offers enrollment in a coeducational class in the same subject, enrollment in a single-sex class is not voluntary. (Federal Register, 2006, p. 62537)

Parents can choose single-gender classes for their child, but coed classes are a guaranteed right. As such, a coed option must be offered. In some schools, an entire grade level or subject area is designated as single-gender. This is permissible, but the principal needs to explain what the coed option would be if requested.

Federal regulations provide guidance for informing parents about their coed option:

If a single-sex class is offered, the recipient is strongly encouraged to notify parents, guardians, and students about their option to enroll in either a single-sex or coeducational class and receive authorization from parents or guardians to enroll their children in a single-sex class. (Federal Register, 2006, p. 62537)

The coed option could be within the existing school or at a different school that offers "substantially equal" classes to the ones offered in the single-gender format. Transportation would need to be provided by the district. The school's leadership team needs to consider how it could provide a coed option within the building. If there are three fourth-grade teachers, one could teach all boys, one all girls, and one coed. If there are five teams of seventh-grade teachers, then at least one could be all boys, at least one all girls, and at least one coed.

Principals who choose to have an entire grade level or subject as single gender would then negotiate a transfer option to a different, but nearby, school. Clearly, this involves coordination among principals and the district office. A parent's satisfaction could be influenced by the perceived quality of the alternative school situation. If a parent insists the coed option at a different school is not acceptable, the district needs to create a coed option at the student's zoned school (which would involve dismantling some of the single-gender program) or disagree and force the student to attend the different school and face possible lawsuit. The courts have not ruled on this issue.

6. Two-Year Review

> *[Requires] the recipient [school] to conduct periodic evaluations to ensure nondiscrimination. (Federal Register, 2006, p. 62531)*
>
> *Evaluations... must be conducted at least every two years. (Federal Register, 2006, p. 62531)*

The final part of the federal regulations is that a single-gender program must be reviewed every two years to ensure nondiscrimination. Reviewing a program involves gathering data that reflect the rationale and educational objective of the program and selection policy. For instance, if a program was created with the goal of increasing academic performance, then academic performance data need to be collected.

The federal regulations require that the data be reviewed. At this time, there is no requirement that the data be reported. However, parents, media, teachers, and the school district most likely will want some feedback after the first year.

SINGLE-SEX SCHOOLS

> *Title IX regulations have permitted single-sex nonvocational schools since the regulations were issued in 1975. (Federal Register, 2006, p. 62540)*
>
> *[Regulation] requires a recipient that operates a public, nonvocational single-sex elementary or secondary school to provide a substantially equal single-sex school or coeducational school to students of the excluded sex. (Federal Register, 2006, p. 62540)*
>
> *The chartering authority will not be required to provide the students of the excluded sex with a substantially equal school. (Federal Register, 2006, p. 62541)*

In addition to single-gender classes and activities, the federal regulations allow for school districts to offer single-gender schools for boys or girls or both. If the district offers an all-boys school, then girls can either attend a coed school or the district can offer an all-girls school, but an all-girls school is not required. Note that all of the schools must be "substantially equal" in terms of course offerings, quality of instruction, quality of teaching staff, etc.

There is an exception, however: Charter schools can be all boy or all girl, and they are not required, under the federal regulations, to provide a coed or single-gender option. Of course, state laws covering charter schools need to be followed as well.

Any additional state laws governing sex discrimination would need to be followed. For example, the superintendent of Boston schools proposed creating an all-boys school and an all-girls school. After she made her announcement, she learned that such discrimination was not permitted by state law. She then proposed exploring single-gender classes (Vaznis, 2008).

CREATING A MASTER SCHEDULE

When creating a master schedule, the program format and total number of teachers assigned to the school will determine the parameters for the schedule.

At this point, complications arise due to single gender. If the program will have single-gender classes for girls and boys, then each class must be taught twice. If there was one pre-algebra class previously scheduled, then there need to be three in a single-gender program, one for boys, one for girls and one coed (see Table 6.1). This course could be taught by one teacher during different periods or by different teachers.

Table 6.1   Impact of a Teacher Having Single-Gender Classes

	1st Period	2nd Period	3rd Period	4th Period
Before Single Gender	Pre-Algebra	Algebra	Algebra	Algebra
Single Gender	Pre-Algebra for Boys	Pre-Algebra for Girls	Pre-Algebra Coed	Algebra

In some cases, there may only be a small number of qualified students to take a certain course, such as honors English. In this case, the principal will need to determine if there will be honors English for boys and honors English for girls, even if there are only ten students in each class, or only coed classes.

Once classes are designated as single gender, teachers are matched with their classes. Teachers can lead both single-gender and coed classes throughout the day or focus on one type. If a teacher is going to teach both genders in a single-gender program, it tends to be easier for the teacher to teach one gender for several periods and then switch to the other gender for the remaining time.

Teachers report that they are more successful when they teach just one gender and do not switch between all-boy and all-girl classes. Teachers are better able to focus on the needs of one gender. However, if this is done, frequent planning sessions for the teachers of boys and girls are necessary to ensure substantially equal lessons.

Using a list of teachers and classes, the master schedule can take shape. For self-contained classes, typically elementary schools, this task is relatively easy. For departmentalized teams or schools, this can be complicated. As the schedule emerges, it is important to make sure that all course offerings can be scheduled and that all boys and girls are able to attend the necessary classes. Typically, the more honors courses or levels of classes, the more difficult the process because every course needs to be taught three times, once for boys, once for girls, and once as coed. It is possible that a school simply does not have enough teachers to teach all the levels offered in the coed schedule.

Elementary School Scheduling

The easiest and most flexible format for an elementary school occurs when there are at least three teachers at the grade level. The most basic self-contained schedule is when teachers teach one grade level, one gender, in all subjects (see Table 6.2).

Table 6.2   Sample Elementary School Schedule, A

Teacher	Schedule
Teacher A	Boys for all subjects all day
Teacher B	Girls for all subjects all day
Teacher C	Coed for all subjects all day

Alternatively, teachers of single-gender classes could also teach one grade level, both genders, and just teach a specific set of subject areas (see Table 6.3).

Table 6.3   Sample Elementary School Schedule, B

Teacher	Morning Schedule	Afternoon Schedule
Teacher A	Boys, Math/Science	Girls, Math/Science
Teacher B	Girls, ELA/Social Studies	Boys, ELA/Social Studies
Teacher C	Coed, Math/Science	Coed, ELA/Social Studies

Another option is to have single-gender teachers teach one grade level, and one gender, as well as a coed group of students (see Table 6.4). Teachers would teach all subject areas. This scheduling option tends to be used when a specific subject is selected for single-gender classes.

Table 6.4   Sample Elementary School Schedule, C

Teacher	Morning Schedule	Afternoon Schedule
Teacher A	Boys, Math/Science	Coed, ELA/Social Studies
Teacher B	Girls, Math/Science	Coed, ELA/Social Studies
Teacher C	Coed, Math/Science	Coed, ELA/Social Studies

Finally, the single-gender teachers could teach two grade levels (hence at least six teachers), just one gender, and a specific subject area (see Table 6.5). This would be used if it is determined that teachers want to teach only one gender and the school is departmentalized.

Table 6.5   Sample Elementary School Schedule, D

Teacher	Morning Schedule	Afternoon Schedule
Teacher A	Boys, Grade Level A, Math/Science	Boys, Grade Level B, Math/Science
Teacher B	Girls, Grade Level A, Math/Science	Girls, Grade Level B, Math/Science

(Continued)

Table 6.5 (Continued)

Teacher	Morning Schedule	Afternoon Schedule
Teacher C	Boys, Grade Level B, ELA/Social Studies	Boys, Grade Level A, ELA/Social Studies
Teacher D	Girls, Grade Level B, ELA/Social Studies	Girls, Grade Level A, ELA/Social Studies
Teacher E	Coed, Grade Level A, Math/Science	Coed, Grade Level B, Math/Science
Teacher F	Coed, Grade Level B, ELA/Social Studies	Coed, Grade Level A, ELA/Social Studies

Middle School Scheduling

At Least Four Teachers per Grade Level: One Teacher per Core Academic Area

Each teacher teaches a boys' class, a girls' class, and coed classes (see Table 6.6). The issue of "substantially equal" does not arise due to all teachers teaching every student. However, flipping between genders as well as coed classes can be taxing on the teacher.

Table 6.6   Sample Middle School Schedule, A

Teacher	1st Period	2nd Period	3rd Period	4th Period
Teacher A	ELA (Boys)	ELA (Girls)	ELA (Coed A)	ELA (Coed B)
Teacher B	SS (Girls)	SS (Boys)	SS (Coed B)	SS (Coed A)
Teacher C	Math (Coed A)	Math (Coed B)	Math (Boys)	Math (Girls)
Teacher D	Science (Coed B)	Science (Coed A)	Science (Girls)	Science (Boys)

Two Teams With Four Teachers per Team: One Single-Gender and One Coed Team

In this format, the teachers would likely be passionate about their teaching environment (either single gender or coed.) (See Table 6.7.) It would be important for the teachers to collaborate across the two teams so that pacing is similar. The issue of "substantially equal" does not arise because the teacher teaches both boys and girls.

Table 6.7   Sample Middle School Schedule, B

Teacher	1st Period	2nd Period	3rd Period	4th Period
Teacher 1A	ELA (Boys A)	ELA (Boys B)	ELA (Girls A)	ELA (Girls B)
Teacher 1B	SS (Boys B)	SS (Boys A)	SS (Girls B)	SS (Girls A)
Teacher 1C	Math (Girls A)	Math (Girls B)	Math (Boys A)	Math (Boys B)
Teacher 1D	Science (Girls B)	Science (Girls A)	Science (Boys B)	Science (Boys A)
Teacher 2A	ELA (Coed)	ELA (Coed)	ELA (Coed)	ELA (Coed)
Teacher 2B	SS (Coed)	SS (Coed)	SS (Coed)	SS (Coed)
Teacher 2C	Math (Coed)	Math (Coed)	Math (Coed)	Math (Coed)
Teacher 2D	Science (Coed)	Science (Coed)	Science (Coed)	Science (Coed)

Two Teams With Four Teachers per Team: One
Boys' and Coed Team, One Girls' and Coed Team

All teachers have single-gender and coed classes (see Table 6.8). Each team teaches a different gender as well as coed classes. Teachers are able to focus on the gender they prefer teaching, which can be a plus for the teachers and students. However, the administration needs to make sure teachers do not overly stereotype students with their room decorations and learning activities. All teachers would need to collaborate frequently to ensure there are "substantially equal" learning opportunities for boys and girls.

Table 6.8   Sample Middle School Schedule, C

Teacher	1st Period	2nd Period	3rd Period	4th Period
Teacher 1A	ELA (Boys A)	ELA (Boys B)	ELA (Coed)	ELA (Coed)
Teacher 1B	SS (Boys B)	SS (Boys A)	SS (Coed)	SS (Coed)
Teacher 1C	Math (Coed)	Math (Coed)	Math (Boys A)	Math (Boys B)
Teacher 1D	Science (Coed)	Science (Coed)	Science (Boys B)	Science (Boys A)
Teacher 2A	ELA (Coed)	ELA (Coed)	ELA (Girls A)	ELA (Girls B)
Teacher 2B	SS (Coed)	SS (Coed)	SS (Girls B)	SS (Girls A)
Teacher 2C	Math (Girls A)	Math (Girls B)	Math (Coed)	Math (Coed)
Teacher 2D	Science (Girls B)	Science (Girls A)	Science (Coed)	Science (Coed)

Two Teams With Four Teachers per Team:
All Teachers on Both Teams Have Boys, Girls, and Coed Classes

This option ensures all students receive "substantially equal" learning opportunities as the teachers are the same for girls, boys, and coed classes (see Table 6.9). However, teachers might face difficulties as they switch some activities for the boys, girls, and coed classes. For instance, the desk arrangement might change for different classes. This can be tiring for some teachers as they try to meet the needs of specific groups. It does not mean that each group has different activities all the time, but often the dynamic in the groups is different.

Table 6.9   Sample Middle School Schedule, D

Teacher	1st Period	2nd Period	3rd Period	4th Period
Teacher 1A	ELA (Boys A)	ELA (Coed)	ELA (Coed)	ELA (Girls B)
Teacher 1B	SS (Coed)	SS (Boys A)	SS (Girls B)	SS (Coed)
Teacher 1C	Math (Girls A)	Math (Coed)	Math (Coed)	Math (Boys B)
Teacher 1D	Science (Coed)	Science (Girls A)	Science (Boys B)	Science (Coed)
Teacher 2A	ELA (Boys B)	ELA (Coed)	ELA (Girls A)	ELA (Coed)
Teacher 2B	SS (Coed)	SS (Boys B)	SS (Coed)	SS (Girls A)
Teacher 2C	Math (Girls B)	Math (Coed)	Math (Boys A)	Math (Coed)
Teacher 2D	Science (Coed)	Science (Girls B)	Science (Coed)	Science (Boys A)

Three Teams With Four Teachers per Team:
One Girls' Team, One Boys' Team, One Coed Team

Each team teaches a different group of students (see Table 6.10). One team teaches all boys all day, another teaches all girls all day, and the final team teaches coed classes all day. It is important when scheduling by teams that the quality of teachers is comparable. It is important that teachers plan together or at least discuss lessons so the boys and girls have "substantially equal" learning opportunities.

Table 6.10   Sample Middle School Schedule, E

Teacher	1st Period	2nd Period	3rd Period	4th Period
Teacher 1A	ELA (Boys A)	ELA (Boys B)	ELA (Boys C)	ELA (Boys D)
Teacher 1B	SS (Boys B)	SS (Boys A)	SS (Boys D)	SS (Boys C)
Teacher 1C	Math (Boys C)	Math (Boys D)	Math (Boys A)	Math (Boys B)
Teacher 1D	Science (Boys D)	Science (Boys C)	Science (Boys B)	Science (Boys A)
Teacher 2A	ELA (Girls A)	ELA (Girls B)	ELA (Girls C)	ELA (Girls D)
Teacher 2B	SS (Girls B)	SS (Girls A)	SS (Girls D)	SS (Girls C)
Teacher 2C	Math (Girls C)	Math (Girls D)	Math (Girls A)	Math (Girls B)
Teacher 2D	Science (Girls D)	Science (Girls C)	Science (Girls B)	Science (Girls A)
Teacher 3A	ELA (Coed)	ELA (Coed)	ELA (Coed)	ELA (Coed)
Teacher 3B	SS (Coed)	SS (Coed)	SS (Coed)	SS (Coed)
Teacher 3C	Math (Coed)	Math (Coed)	Math (Coed)	Math (Coed)
Teacher 3D	Science (Coed)	Science (Coed)	Science (Coed)	Science (Coed)

High School Scheduling

In high schools, teachers teach different courses that may be on different grade levels. As such, the variety of schedules is too numerous to list. The process really involves matching the number of students who enroll in a class (single gender or coed) and determining if that class will have enough students to be on the master schedule.

If a ninth-grade academy concept is used, then scheduling can follow the middle school schedule with at least four teachers per team.

CHAPTER 6 PLANNING TOOL: EXAMINING LEGAL BOUNDARIES AND SCHEDULE RESTRAINTS

Explain how your program will meet each of the legal points:

1. The program must have an "important educational objective."
   What data will you use?
   What will your objective be?

2. The program must be "completely voluntary."
   Which selection process will you use (opt in or opt out)?
   Describe the process.
   How will you provide parents the option to opt out?

3. The program must be "substantially equal" for boys and girls within single gender as compared to coed.
   How will you ensure classes are "substantially equal"?
   Will you review lesson plans?
   Will you conduct classroom observations?
   Will you review teaching or assessment documents?

4. The program can be for boys only, for girls only, or for boys and girls.
   Who will be eligible for the program?
   Is this supported by your data and rationale?

5. The program must have a coed option available.
   What is your coed option?
   Is it at your school?
   If at a different school, does the superintendent support this?

6. The program must be reviewed every two years to determine if it is nondiscriminatory and addresses the educational rationale.
   What data will you use to review your program?
   How often will these data be collected?
   Who will review the data?
   Who will write the statement?
   What will you do if there are concerns and issues?

- Which sample schedule can serve as a starting point for your single-gender program?

   Use the table below to draft your own schedule.

7

Communication

C hange is often difficult. People can be resistant regardless of positive intentions or a noble purpose. Single-gender programs are no different. In fact, single-gender program proposals often experience high levels of suspicion. Establishing early, open, and honest lines of communication is essential to clear up misunderstandings. Regardless of the starting point for a single-gender program, each group must be brought into the fold, their ideas gathered and considered, their questions addressed, and ultimately a clear vision for the program established that all can support. There are five key groups for communication: (1) principal (or school administration), (2) teachers, (3) parents, (4) students, and (5) school board members.

Each of those groups has the power to create the program as well as end it. The principal supports a program with materials and professional development funds. Teachers are the ones who breathe life into the program. Their commitment to the program and confidence in delivering it will make or break the program. The parents are either satisfied or not by the program. They will choose to be a part of it or not. Parents will talk with other parents and build up or take down the program. Students are the ones in the program and their attitude toward the program and performance within the program will ultimately determine its continuation. The school board, of course, has the ultimate veto on the program.

Importantly, all groups should receive the same information regarding rationale, policy, and procedures throughout the process, though different information may be emphasized and expanded for different groups.

This chapter provides suggestions for what to emphasize with each group during the implementation phase. A recommended pace for informing each group is provided at the end of this chapter. Suggestions for sustaining a program are the subject of the final chapter, Chapter 12, "Sustaining a Single-Gender Program."

COMMUNICATION WITH PRINCIPALS AND SCHOOL ADMINISTRATORS

> [Dayton, Ohio] Superintendent Percy Mack said the district wants to give parents more educational choices for their children because research shows boys and girls learn differently. "We have to develop strategies to accommodate those learning differences in young people," Mack said. (Kissell, 2005, p. B1, B4)

In today's high-stakes testing environment, principals need to know how single-gender programs can improve student achievement and the school's report card rating. New programs or changes to the school need to have the potential to improve the school's rating (i.e., academic performance of students). As such, it is critical that a teacher or parent trying to pitch the idea of single gender to a principal be prepared with data from public schools with single-gender programs (see Chapter 2). Another source of data is news articles from across the country. While formal longitudinal studies are likely to begin in the near future, data do not exist at this time to show the long-term results of single-gender programs in public school. Educators must rely on self-reported results or media observations.

Principals also need to know that they can start a single-gender program incrementally. They do not need to turn a whole school into a single-gender school to be successful. Principals know their parent community and know how it will likely react to change. Some schools are known for being innovative and trying new programs and strategies, and are supported by their parent community. Other schools are known for providing certain features that are the bedrock of the entire school and change may take more time. A single-gender program can find a home in each of these environments, and it can start small and grow as its success builds. It is unwise to put a single-gender program in place simply to have the appearance of being cutting edge or innovative if the school community isn't behind it.

The most difficult issue for principals will probably be scheduling, discussed in detail in Chapter 6. Principals tend to either create or approve the master schedule for their schools. They need to be aware that making a schedule within a single-gender program can be difficult depending on their goals, willing teachers, and interested parents.

COMMUNICATION WITH TEACHERS

Teachers need to know that single-gender education is really a form of differentiated instruction. Carol Ann Tomlinson (2003), author of multiple resources on differentiated instruction, states:

> In fact, because students do differ so greatly, the premise of differentiation is that while students have the same *basic* needs, those needs will *manifest themselves* in different ways, depending on the student's gender, culture, general life experiences, talents, interests, learning preferences, affective development, cognitive development, and support systems. (p. 19)

As with differentiated instruction, students in single-gender programs are responsible for the content and skills required by their state or district curriculum; however, the way in which the content and skills are taught can be different. Presenting single-gender education as a form of differentiated instruction often eases teachers' fears that single gender is another set of trainings, worksheets, lesson plan formats, and paperwork that needs to be completed, and then abandoned the following year. Teachers are suspicious of new programs. Presenting news articles or survey responses about single-gender programs to teachers can provide a positive context for teachers. For example, many teachers of single-gender classes say that they are able to spend more time teaching and less time managing student misbehavior.

Learning about single-gender education requires commitment. There can be a steep learning curve, particularly in the beginning as teachers learn about recent research about gender differences. Teacher training is critical in order to make a smooth transition into single-gender education. Teachers need to commit to training organized by the school, district, or state; participate in a book study; and engage in ongoing group reflection about their lessons, strategies, and students. While there are no lesson plans that are for boys only or girls only (nor should there be), there are procedures that tend to work well with boys and with girls. Utilizing this information with their own lesson plans and reflecting on the impact will strengthen the single-gender program (and can also be used with teachers of coed classes). This process is important with any new educational program, but again, with single-gender it is critical. The issue of professional development is specifically addressed in Chapter 11.

Initial information for the teachers typically takes place through a faculty meeting. Usually, there will be several faculty meetings at which gender and single-gender education is discussed. At first, data about student achievement and discipline by gender should be presented and single gender offered as one option. At another meeting, more information about gender differences can be introduced and initial interest of teachers teaching in single-gender classes can be gauged. More formal training then occurs through the professional development plan.

COMMUNICATION WITH PARENTS

> Parent Rebecca Windham was irate when the classes were separated at midyear. Her son was doing fine, and she feared that his performance would suffer once the girls were removed. "I didn't like my kid being used as a guinea pig," she said. "I went in there thinking this was going to be a sexual-discrimination suit. But once I saw the test scores, I was proved wrong." (Klein & Owens, 2006, p. A8)

Communication with parents is critical and often overlooked. Parents need to know that the school administration is considering single-gender education because the school believes it is in the best interest of the children. Parents will want to know why a program is being considered. Presenting data regarding student achievement and behavior can provide the basis for creating a program. Discussing the program rationale with parents often strengthens their buy-in to the program.

Parents also need to know that the single-gender program is a choice, even if the school plans on designating a whole grade level or subject area as single-gender classes. In all forms of communication, the school needs to be sure to explain the coed option for the parents. Sample letters to parents are included in Resources F–I.

Parents can become enthusiastic about single-gender options through hearing success stories from other programs in their state and across the nation. This way, administrators and teachers are able to show themselves as working within an established educational alternative and not as conducting a high-risk experiment.

A school or district might provide a workshop where parents can learn about differences between boys and girls, and, more importantly, how teachers use this information to meet the needs of their students.

Finally, parents should be informed as to the procedures of the program, specifically the selection process and timeline for implementation. Parents will opt to have their child be a part of a single-gender program for many different reasons. Some will see the value of the learning opportunities available within a single-gender environment. Others will see it as a chance for their child to be better understood. One parent explained, "My child [a first grade boy] doesn't need to take his medication this year now that he is in a single-gender class with a teacher who understands his needs more and is able to work with him." Parents may also see single-gender classes as a chance to help socialize their child. A mother was grateful that her son's school created single-gender classes and that her son was a part of the program. Her reason, "He has two sisters, a mother, and a female dog. Dad is a soldier in the Middle East. My son needs some male influence."

The comfort level of a child is one of the main factors for parents choosing a single-gender class. A teacher recalled a note she received the first week of school when starting an all-girls, fifth-grade class, "The parent was so thankful her daughter was in a single-gender class. She [daughter] has two prosthetic legs and this was the first year her child did not come home crying and hating school because of something a boy said or did. She is thriving." We cannot presume we know all the reasons that parents may opt for a single-gender program. What we can do is provide the best opportunity possible.

Initial communication with parents can be made through the school newsletter. Parents whose child could be affected by the single-gender program should be contacted by written communication. A follow-up meeting to explain the program and answer questions should take place. Opportunities to meet with the principal during the year regarding the implementation of a single-gender program (or any program) should take place periodically.

COMMUNICATION WITH STUDENTS

Having a teacher who understands that girls and boys are different is the best part. And my single-gender teacher treats everybody the same, no matter what race they are.

—Sixth-grade girl

The best part is if I had something to say, I could say it without offending a female.

—Eighth-grade boy

Before the program begins, students will hear about the program through their parents, informational fliers, and other students. Oftentimes, students attend parent meetings with their parents. Students may react strongly and negatively because they do not want a change. They may also wait to react until they talk with their friends and see who is interested in which format. In either case, students need to know why the program is being established and that it is about helping them succeed, not ruining their social life.

The student government is a good place to begin the conversation about single-gender education. It is critical to stress the potential benefits of being in a single-gender program to students as they may be quick to see separation from peers as a negative. Potential benefits should reflect the rationale for creating the program, and can include more focus on academics, fewer distractions and discipline issues, and increased opportunity for participation. Clearly explaining the schedule for students—when they would have single-gender classes, coed classes, and time to interact with the opposite sex—is important for decreasing their potential anxiety.

Administrators should give students a chance to voice their concerns and questions so that they do not rebel against the program because it is a perceived forced decision by the school. Focus groups with students in different grade levels could be organized, and then could meet with selected administrators during different lunch periods. Clearing any misconceptions and considering students' perspectives will give strength to the single-gender program launch.

As the program is implemented, it is important to encourage students to give feedback and voice their concerns and suggestions. A simple survey asking students about their satisfaction, best parts, and parts to improve could be distributed after the first quarter of the program. Often, students may see the benefits of single-gender classes but want students of the opposite sex in the class for socialization.

Communication with students tends to be most effective during meetings with food. Merely sending out written information or posting information without any face-to-face time leads to differing interpretations circulating around the school.

COMMUNICATION WITH SCHOOL BOARD MEMBERS

Principals know the degree to which board members tend to be concerned about the specific details of a new program. However, school board members are ultimately responsible for approving or denying a program. There are four key pieces of information to present to the school board.

First, the school board needs to know that single-gender education is legal. Board members will want to know who will take legal responsibility for following the federal regulations. At the very least, the board will ask that the school district's attorney review all single-gender program plans. The school board should only approve a school plan that involves single-gender classes across a whole grade or subject area for all students if there is a coed option at another school. Remember that this single-gender structure will require, by the federal regulations, transportation provided by the district to the coed school.

Second, the board will want to know the cost of the new program. Single-gender programs require minimal additional funding, as explained in detail in Chapter 9.

Third, like the parents, the school board will want to know about other single-gender programs and their successes and difficulties. Many of these programs have been highlighted in news reports across the country. Articles are available with simple searches via the Internet.

Fourth, every school board likes positive public relations. The media is very quick to cover events that involve single-gender programs. Recent stories have been positive as they relate the successes of the programs and share observations from teachers, parents, and students.

It is necessary to keep the school board informed as the program is implemented. The board will want to know how many parents opted out of the program, if the program is "full," and if students are happy and successful. Achievement data may not be available until later in the school year, but anecdotal accounts from students, parents, and teachers can be gathered and provided. Communication with the school board will also often involve a written summary or statement as well as a short presentation during a monthly board meeting.

ORDER OF CONCERNS IN COMMUNICATING WITH EACH GROUP

It is important not to overwhelm groups with information or be perceived as having the final decision already determined and their input not matter. As such, providing information to each group at a reasonable pace is important. Table 7.1 shows a recommended order in which information can be provided to each group, depending on their primary concerns. ("POST" indicates information provided after the program is implemented.)

Table 7.1   Pace of Providing Information to Stakeholders

Principals and Administrators	Teachers	Parents	Students	School Board Members
❑ Rationale ❑ Need (Data)	❑ Rationale ❑ Need (Data) ❑ Definition	❑ Rationale ❑ Definition ❑ Benefits ❑ Choice Option	❑ Rationale ❑ Definition ❑ Benefits	❑ Rationale ❑ Need (Data)
❑ Schedule Options	❑ Research on Gender Differences	❑ Research on Gender Differences ❑ Students' Experiences in the Classroom	❑ Schedule ❑ Learning Options ❑ Students' Experiences in the Classroom	❑ Structure ❑ Policies
❑ Feedback ❑ Anecdotal Information	❑ Opportunities for Single-Gender Education ❑ Schedule Ideas	❑ Structure ❑ Selection Process ❑ Choice ❑ Policies	❑ Question and Answer	**POST** ❑ Anecdotal Information

(Continued)

Table 7.1 (Continued)

Principals and Administrators	Teachers	Parents	Students	School Board Members
❑ Data Based on Rationale	❑ Question and Answer ❑ Feedback ❑ Reflection on Practice	❑ Question and Answer	**POST** ❑ Feedback	**POST** ❑ Data Based on Rationale ❑ Future Plans
	POST ❑ Feedback ❑ Future Plans	**POST** ❑ Feedback ❑ Future Plans	**POST** ❑ Future Plans	

AVOIDING STEREOTYPES

Finally, in all communication about single gender, with every group of stakeholders, it is critical that educators not stereotype boys and girls by saying "all boys" or "all girls" learn in only one exclusive way; or that boys move around a lot, and girls sit still, listen, and do their work; or that boys are naturally good at math and girls are naturally verbal. Characterizing gender differences in this way limits the opportunities for students.

Accomplishing this can be a difficult task. Much of the recent media and popular books tend to frame boys and girls as opposites. Think Mars and Venus. Consider the saying, "Boys will be boys." In earlier writings about gender, it was often said that boys have greater abilities in spatial reasoning and girls in verbal abilities. Phrasing the conversation in terms of predetermined abilities signifies that the other gender has no hope of learning those skills. This certainly is not the case as evidenced by the improvement of female performance in mathematics.

The school and district community needs to determine their agreement and comfort level with recent research on brain-based and hormone gender differences that were touched upon in Chapter 1. While these differences should not be the reason for creating a single-gender program, as mentioned earlier, they certainly could be used to inform the practice of teachers. And, this information can help inform teachers of single-gender classes as well as coed classes. Gender is not just a single-gender education issue. And stereotyping does not exist solely in single-gender classes. Communicating this research is important as it will likely affect the teaching practices of the teachers and learning opportunities of students.

CHAPTER 7 PLANNING TOOL: PREPARING FOR COMMUNICATION

Use this checklist to make sure you have what you need for your presentation to each group.

Principals and School Administrators	Teachers	Parents	Students	School Board Members
❑ Date of Initial Announcement _____	❑ Date of Initial Announcement _____	❑ Date of Initial Announcement _____	❑ Date of Initial Announcement _____	❑ Date of Initial Announcement _____
❑ Data	❑ Data	❑ Choice	❑ Benefits	❑ Legal
❑ Articles	❑ Articles	❑ Policies	❑ Schedule	❑ Cost
❑ Scheduling Ideas	❑ Research on Gender and Learning	❑ Data	❑ Choice	❑ Articles
		❑ Articles		
		❑ Research on Gender and Learning		

8

Building Community

Single-gender education is about separating boys and girls into different classrooms, but teaching them the same curriculum, holding them accountable for learning, and holding them to appropriate behavioral expectations. In prior chapters, several issues regarding the creation of a single-gender program were discussed; it is time now to consider the community being created.

INTEGRATION OF SINGLE-GENDER PROGRAMS INTO SCHOOL CULTURE

Before moving forward, administrators must decide how they want to introduce a single-gender program. Will there be special meetings, press releases, or promotions? Or, will the program quietly come into existence, blending into the other programs at the school? Either way works, but plans should be made before groups start going in different directions.

Recognize that the very creation of a single-gender class will create a degree of difficulty for students because the program is new and involves separation. Denying that this will happen can lead to misperceptions about the program and how it fits within the school as a whole. At a minimum, the whole school community should be made aware of the great learning opportunities at the school, including single-gender classes. There are two basic ways to go about this.

1.   Some schools use the creation of a single-gender program as an opportunity to make students involved feel special and a part of something important. Perhaps the students in the single-gender program have not been recognized for accomplishments in the past in academics, sports, or clubs—the single-gender program offers them a unique opportunity. If so, having some fanfare with the creation of a single-gender program may be warranted.

2.   Other schools choose to present the program as simply one of multiple programs available at the school. Principals explain all programs available to parents and students via newsletters, morning announcements, or news shows and back-to-school nights. New programs or procedures, including single gender, would be explained but not necessarily singled out more than others. Perhaps the student newspaper or news program could highlight one of the new programs with each issue.

Both options provide opportunities for the school to alleviate fears, concerns, and questions about the program. Often, students want to feel connected to their program. Indeed, students are a part of a state, district, and school, but in their daily interactions, they will often be referred to by their program or team. Demystifying this identification will lay the groundwork for a positive learning experience.

IDENTITY OF THE SINGLE-GENDER PROGRAM

Once a community understands how the single-gender program relates to the whole school, it will be important to determine how the program will identify itself. In some cases, students are recruited to create the identity of their program as a way of building community and ownership. There are several important questions to consider with identity.

Will your single-gender program have a unique name? Creating a name has strong and weak points. For example, the name TWO Academies plays on the idea that there are two academies, one for boys and one for girls. Names can also represent the rationale for creating the program, such as the Renewed Opportunity Center for Kids (ROCK) and Excellence in Creativity and Educational Leadership (EXCEL). Some program names reflect the school name and mascot.

Identifying your program with a particular name can create a bond for the members. However, once a group is identified, they may no longer feel part of other groups. This could lead to an "us vs. them" mentality. Administrators should decide what is appropriate for their school, considering the students' ages. Keep in mind that if administrators don't name the program, students may themselves label the program, whether in positive or negative ways.

If the program does not have a name, students can adopt a name for their class. For example, one elementary school located near the coast incorporates sea themes across the school, and the single-gender classes were called The Mermaids and The Orcas.

Will your program have a logo? If so, will there be one for boys and one for girls? The logo often comes from the program's name or is related to the school mascot. For example, if the school mascot is the dolphin, then program logos could include other marine animals or locations where dolphins live. If the school mascot is the eagle, then the program name and logos could reflect different types of eagles.

Will your program have a motto? A motto summarizes why the program exists as well as its goals. Acronyms such as R.O.C.K. create their own motto by identifying what each letter represents. The TWO Academies uses the motto "Maximizing Potential" as a way to state that the program focuses on educating the whole child.

Will your program have unique items for its students? These items can include T-shirts, car magnets, notebooks, and stationery. This has the benefit of creating an image for the group and an aura of importance. This can be very helpful as a program starts. It can aid in program recognition throughout the community and establish pride among the participants. However, it can also be perceived as snobbish, and that can be detrimental to the program.

LOCATION OF SINGLE-GENDER CLASSES

Will the single-gender program be housed in the current classrooms or in a location unto itself? The benefit of integration is that the students can interact when not in their classrooms.

Having a unique location helps students relate to others who are in the single-gender program, and the teachers are able to communicate more effectively. This would build community among students and teachers. Hallways can be decorated to promote the single-gender program successes of all members and reinforces its priorities and goals. Of course, the negative could be that the students don't feel as part of the whole school. The teachers may also feel isolated and shunned by the other teachers. This is not inevitable, though, if the principal has incorporated the single-gender program into the school as a whole.

PROGRAM CREED

Creeds are designed to express the program's purpose and expectations. Creating a creed is helpful for any school, club, or group of students. A creed for a single-gender program is something that can take a decidedly gendered slant for boys and for girls based upon the rationale for creating the program. As such, it builds a sense of community for all involved. Creeds in single-gender programs should reflect the same mission of the school. However, some programs may want to have specifics that differ for boys or girls, or have posters that explain what the creed can mean for boys and what the creed can mean for girls.

Creeds can be recited at the beginning of the day or at the beginning of class as a way to focus the students on the opportunities they will be offered. This could help students who are teased for being in a single-gender program. The creed allows students to reaffirm their commitment to the program. Two creeds are located in Resource A at the back of the book. Urban Prep, an all-boys public high school in Chicago, started in 2002, created and adopted "The Creed," which is posted on their Web site (www.urbanprep.org) and recited every day.

PUBLIC RELATIONS PLAN

The concept of single-gender classes is new enough that the media finds it interesting. As such, the local media often come to schools starting single-gender programs, with or without an invitation. Therefore, each school must be ready for them with information and answers to their questions. The media can also be a powerful avenue for building community. Seeing oneself or one's program in the newspaper can create a sense of pride.

Being proactive is the best course of action. The administration can invite the press to visit the school during training sessions, the first day of school, or events that involve the single-gender students. If additional positive media coverage is desired, any field study, speaker, or fundraising effort within the single-gender program can become a media event. However, having too much media coverage for the single-gender program can create ill feelings among other staff members who may feel they are doing just as much work with no publicity. In addition, teachers in the single-gender program might not want the attention; they might just want to teach.

Depending on the situation, neither of those may happen. But if they do, an administrator can calm the waters by pointing out that the single-gender program is new and that makes news, and by emphasizing that the media attention of the single-gender program could be stimulus for other teachers or programs to be highlighted.

COORDINATOR FOR THE
SINGLE-GENDER PROGRAM

At some point, a coordinator for single-gender programs needs to be designated. There are multiple tasks that need to be addressed throughout the year in order to keep the program moving forward and successful. Assuming that "someone" will handle these details can lead to the details being forgotten. This can break down staff commitment and student desire to remain in the program. Depending on the breadth of implementation within a district, there may need to be two positions, one at the district level and one at the school.

The district coordinator ensures consistent communication from the district to the schools, including procedures for starting a program, handling of media, coordination of teacher training, facilitating visits to schools and among schools, collecting overall data, evaluating teachers and programs, coordinating meetings of teachers in single-gender programs, and responding to parent concerns. These duties can initially be given to an administrator with similar duties, such as director of professional development or director of special programs. Of course, if there are multiple schools involved in single-gender programs, a separate position might be warranted.

Importantly, the district coordinator has the task of making sure single-gender programs begin in the strongest way and comply with federal regulations. With a district coordinator, a school would not be allowed to start a program without going through steps designated by the district. In fact, a single-gender program proposal form could be used as a way to regulate who is doing what. An example of a Single-Gender Proposal Form is included in Resource B.

The school coordinator would be the conduit for single-gender issues for the school, including media, parents, and teachers. In addition to performing similar duties as the district coordinator, the school coordinator can assist with scheduling, promotional material, setting up field studies or guest speakers, checking lesson plans, gathering resources for teachers, and facilitating collaboration among teachers. Typically, these duties fall to the principal, assistant principal, or curriculum facilitator. It is important to be respectful of the number of tasks an administrator is expected to perform. In addition, asking a teacher to perform these tasks in addition to her regular teaching load is likely too much. Some schools provide a stipend or additional planning period for a teacher who takes on the role of coordinator.

In both cases, district and school coordinators are important for a vital single-gender program. Certainly, the programs can exist initially through the support of a principal or leadership team, but it is the details and the daily support that allow the program to continue. In South Carolina, there is a statewide coordinator for single-gender initiatives.

TEAM BUILDING FOR STUDENTS

Many schools start their day with homeroom. In most cases, this is an opportunity to hear announcements and get ready for the day. Some schools also have an advisory period, circle time, or morning meeting when staff members work with small groups of students on study skills, guidance issues, or social issues. It is imperative that schools with single-gender programs find time in their schedule to work with their students in single-gender programs. Groups of all boys and all girls need to learn how to work together as a group. This may seem obvious, but many schools put boys together and girls together and expect them to magically get along in their single-gender groupings. Single-gender classes might eliminate cross-gender distractions among boys and girls, but there are still potential issues for all boys and all girls.

Creating a weekly time, possibly fifteen minutes, when teachers can work with students and address any issues can greatly strengthen the overall single-gender program and benefit time on-task within the classroom. Team-building activities and friendship discussions are easy to implement and allow students to learn how to work together. Used weekly, or more, they help build group cohesion. During team-building activities, the group has to complete a task that involves every person. For example, "mission impossible" or "new games" activities involve students getting from one end of a room or space outside to the other end using only a limited number of items (e.g., a board, three cans, and broom handle). In addition, the ground is lava and the whole group returns to the starting point if any one of them touches the ground. Other activities involve the group trying to reach a group goal or point level and everyone has the chance to contribute. For instance, the group has to earn as many points as possible by hitting a beach ball in the air. Points are gained with one point for hitting the ball with a hand, two for the head, and three for bouncing the ball with feet. The two rules are that a player cannot hit the ball two times consecutively and the ball cannot touch the ground, wall, ceiling, etc. The group works very hard trying to reach their goal and do their personal best. Members can get frustrated, but with teacher facilitation, they realize that if they do not encourage each other, they will not be able to reach their goal. This translates back into the classroom as students work together to complete class activities and small-group projects. The lesson plan for this activity is located in Resource C.

Another use of meeting time is for students to address friendship issues before they become problems. Students can write down a situation in which they became angry or hurt by another person. The situations are then categorized by the teacher or students, and the teacher selects one for students to role-play bettering better or worse scenarios. While the group of students is acting out the situation, the teacher and other students write down the trigger words and actions (shrugs, looks, gestures, etc.) that make the situation worse and better. Teachers can then post these lists and use them as resources for helping students make positive choices.

Incorporating a character education program or guidance program during this time is also beneficial, but not necessary. Community service could be planned during these times as well. Mentoring opportunities may also be incorporated with older students working with younger students as reading buddies, science lab partners, or math consultants. The key is to give students the chance to be involved in engaging activities that benefit them as people and students, as well as to create a sense of community.

CHAPTER 8 PLANNING TOOL: CREATING COMMUNITY

Use the following checklist of questions to help you build a strong community.

School Culture

- ❑ How many programs operate within your school?
- ❑ Do any of them have a distinct way of identifying themselves?
- ❑ Do any of them have special evening sessions, presentations, etc.?
- ❑ Why would it be beneficial for the single-gender program to be identified as a unique program?
- ❑ How would it hurt the program or students to be identified as a unique program?

Identification of Program

- ❑ Does your school have a motto, logo, or mascot?
- ❑ Could the single-gender program be derived from any of these?
- ❑ What are some related names of the school mascot that could be used by the single-gender program?

Location

- ❑ Could teachers be moved in order to place the single-gender classrooms together?
- ❑ Could teachers be moved in order to place the single-gender classrooms in each grade level together?
- ❑ What is the downside and upside of moving teachers?
- ❑ Could teachers of other programs be moved in order to be together?

Creed

- ❑ What is your goal for students in the single-gender program?
- ❑ How can these ideas come together in a creed?

Public Relations

Do you want media attention?

- ❑ Are the media positive about education in your city or district?
- ❑ Are teachers at your school comfortable with the media?
- ❑ What kind of media attention has your school received in the past?

Coordinator

❑ Who is the logical person to be the point person for the single-gender program?

❑ Does this person (or small group) have the time to make the single-gender program successful?

❑ What else is this person responsible for?

❑ Are there funds to support this position?

Team Building for Students

❑ When can there be a time for students to do team-building activities?

❑ Does a program already exist at the school that helps build community among students?

❑ Are there mentoring or community service opportunities available?

❑ What other opportunities are there for students to build community?

9

Program Price

Creating single-gender classes and schools can be done essentially without additional funding. Schools across the country are implementing single-gender classes within schools using existing teachers and materials.

LOW-COST OPTIONS

The lowest-cost option for a single-gender program is when a principal designates a certain number of sections or classes at the school as single-gender with no additional teachers or resources. For example, instead of a teacher having four coed classes of sixth-grade science, the teacher has one boys' class, one girls' class, and two coed classes.

A school district could even designate two elementary or middle schools as single gender, with one being all boys and the other being all girls, provided that there is an additional elementary or middle school available as coed.

Turning two coed schools into two single-gender schools (one all boys and one all girls) involves all of the issues described in this book and can have additional logistical tasks of student placement and transportation. However, in theory, the principal, teachers, and materials remain the same, hence little additional cost. In practice, the creation of single-sex schools takes significant time to find a location, communicate with the community, and have a smooth transition.

All options, however, involve communication costs. Letters of notification about single-gender classes, information packets about the program, and postage for sending the letters and packets should be included in the budget. But this information can be included within regularly scheduled mailings. If a school or district wants to draw particular attention to the single-gender program, then separate mailings are needed.

Though not advisable, it is possible and legal to implement single-gender education without providing professional development. Professional development is discussed in Chapter 10, but here it is important to point out that schools and districts should allocate some of their professional development budget to the training and support of teachers within single-gender classes.

MODERATE-COST OPTIONS

More than likely, a school or district will invest some resources to create a single-gender program. The immediate costs will be professional development and training. Conducting book studies helps to introduce the idea of gender differences to teachers, and this involves purchasing sets of books for teachers. Sending teams of faculty to visit schools with single-gender programs involves travel expenses as well as substitute pay (and the hidden cost of taking the teacher from the classroom for a day or two). Hiring a consultant to provide onsite training involves fees and expenses. But all of these options provide knowledge that can benefit the entire school, not just teachers involved with single gender.

For example, in Florida, grant funds were provided to support schools starting single-gender programs. A local newspaper reported:

Sample Professional Development Costs

$400 Book Study (twenty teachers at a time)

- $20 per book = $400

$1,520 Two-Day Site Visit (five teachers by car)

- Substitute Pay: $70 per day = $140/Teacher x 5 = $700
- Travel (1 car/van): 300 miles roundtrip @ .50 per mile = $150
- Meals: 5 teachers x $37 per diem x 2 days = $370
- Lodging: 3 rooms (assume 2 doubles and 1 single) x $100 per room = $300

$6,000 On-Site Training

- Consultant Fee = $5,000 per day
- Travel Expenses (air, hotel, meals, car) = $1,000

Manatee school officials began toying with the idea of same-sex classes when the state of Florida started offering grants for schools to pilot these classes. Last year's Florida Comprehensive Assessment Test scores show that in Manatee County, the third-, fourth- and fifth-grade girls surpassed their male counterparts in reading and writing, according to the Florida Department of Education. The boys outscored the girls in math. So the district last year applied and received a $40,000 state grant to pilot single-sex classes. That money was used to train teachers. (Lim, 2007, p. 1A)

The reason that single-gender remains a relatively cost-effective reform movement is that there are no program or package costs at this time. A school does not have to purchase a set of materials, workbooks, training sessions, and equipment to implement single-gender education.

HIGH-COST OPTIONS

Although single-gender programs can be implemented for little or moderate cost, it is certainly possible to spend large amounts of money on creating a program. Three types of costs may be involved: facilities, transportation, and training. Many single-gender programs start small and grow, adding classes or grade levels each year. Continued training is a cost. Finding a location that will be large enough down the road might not be cost-effective in the beginning because of the lower population, but would eventually incur a significant expense. Large amounts of money could also be spent on consultants to provide initial training, follow-up training, and classroom visits with feedback for teachers. There are even organizations that offer services to review curriculums in light of boys and girls. Of course, this is not required and can be accomplished using current personnel in the school or district. However, it is an option to hire a consultant on a long-term basis.

Creating a new single-gender school involves substantial costs, but most of these costs are related to creating a new school and not necessarily due to the single-gender format. There are some organizations that financially support school options, particularly single gender. The Cleveland and George Gund foundations gave the city of Cleveland school district $300,000 to establish four single-gender elementary schools, two for girls and two for boys. Each of the schools eventually will have prekindergarten–eighth grade, but they all started with prekindergarten–second grade and add a grade each year. In Texas, the Young Woman's Leadership Organization partners with school districts to establish schools for girls. The organization provides $1 million over a four-year period to support enhancements for all-girls schools, and to date they have partnered to open four public all-girls schools.

Hiring Additional Teachers

A large cost for implementing a single-gender program, or any program, is hiring additional teachers. This cost will arise if the school wants to have smaller classes or if a school has leveled classes and offers those classes only once in the schedule, such as an Algebra I class or an honors English class. Then, the school may need to hire an additional teacher to make those classes single gender and still be able to offer a coed option as required by federal regulations.

Consider a school where there are twenty students in an Algebra I class (say ten boys and ten girls) and this class is offered only once a term. In this case, making it single gender would require the school to triple the number of times it was taught; once for boys and once for girls (and be able to offer a coed option). As a result, if the school wants to provide single-gender Algebra I classes, it might hire an additional teacher to teach just one class so that the overall schedule is not affected adversely, or hire the teacher to teach a full load and reduce class sizes across several sections. Remember, a teacher must have a classroom in which to teach. This could mean that a portable classroom would be needed or that the teacher would float among available classrooms. These issues point to the reason why many principals do not offer single-gender options for classes that are historically offered only once per term at the school. Nonetheless, hiring an additional teacher to provide scheduling flexibility within a single-gender program, and across the whole school, is an option.

Organizations for the Learning of Boys and Girls

Center for the Study of Boys' and Girls' Lives
www.csbl.org

Chadwell Consulting
www.chadwellconsulting.com

Coalition of Schools Educating Boys of Color
www.coseboc.org

The Deak Group
www.deakgroup.com

The Gurian Institute
www.gurianinstitute.org

International Boys School Coalition
www.theibsc.org

National Association for Single-Sex Public Education
www.nasspe.org

National Coalition of Girls' Schools
www.ncgs.org

Rockhouse Associates
www.rockhouseassociates.org

Rosalind Wiseman
www.rosalindwiseman.com

Hiring a Coordinator

The other cost for single gender is hiring a coordinator for the program. As discussed previously, having a contact person for the single-gender program is beneficial for parents, students, teachers, and the community—someone to provide information to parents and the media, answer questions, and gather resources for teachers of single-gender classes and the whole school. This person could also conduct classroom observations and gather professional development resources for

Adding a Single-Gender Program to a School: The TWO Academies, Columbia, SC

The TWO Academies started as a magnet program at Dent Middle School in the summer of 2004. It was a new program at the school, not replacing any program or causing a reorganization of the overall schedule. To make this happen, four portable classrooms were rented and four teachers were hired, one each for mathematics, English language arts, science, and social studies. Two administrators were hired to oversee the program, one for boys and one for girls. Desks, computers, textbooks, and resources were purchased. Essentially, the program followed a school-within-a-school model.

The following year, four additional classrooms and materials were purchased, and four additional teachers hired in order to expand to seventh grade. The year after that, another four classrooms, materials, and teachers were needed as the program expanded to eighth grade. The final location for the program became a wing of the school once renovations were finished. The core academic classes for all sixth, seventh, and eighth grades occurred in the same area, and students go "out" for lunch and related arts, and to the media center, nurse, computer lab, and other typical school needs.

teachers. While this could be a separate position, it could also be an additional task for existing personnel or even a teacher if a stipend and additional planning time are provided.

There are other costs that could cause a budget to rise. Teachers should conduct a book inventory and determine if they have enough books that boys and girls tend to enjoy. If not, they could purchase books related to a particular genre to better meet the interests of students.

Schools may also want to capitalize on the single-gender environment to ensure that all students have access to technology. As such, they may purchase additional technology resources for the classroom (i.e., SmartBoard or Promethean Boards, laptop computers, or digital equipment). Though not necessarily designated as a single-gender issue, student interests and ability with technology is an important issue that has a possible gender component when one looks at career projections, especially for females in science, technology, engineering, and mathematics.

Another area with a possible single-gender component is for teachers to arrange for speakers and field studies related to issues of leadership or character. Teachers already invite speakers to their classes, have career days, and arrange for field study experiences to give students hands-on experiences. In addition to these traditional activities, teachers may seek out speakers who can challenge stereotypes of being male and female. For example, Jean Toal is the chief justice for the South Carolina Supreme Court, and arranging for Chief Justice Toal to speak to the students in single-gender groups would be worthwhile learning experiences for both the boys and the girls. For the girls, this experience provides examples of what they can become. For the boys, this experience shows them what is possible for girls, dismissing stereotypes about girls and women. In terms of financial costs, transportation would need to be calculated for field studies, and guest speaker fees would need to be budgeted.

Principals may also want to physically restructure their school to accommodate the program, which would include adding classroom space, classroom furniture (including new types of desks and tables), teaching materials, and teachers. Needless to say, this involves considerable costs.

There is also the option of creating a single-gender charter school, which is allowed under federal guidelines. However, charter school organizations need to check state laws, as some deny single-gender options. If all-boys or all-girls schools are not allowed, then the dual academy approach could be used. This is a high-cost option due to the facility and personnel needs, but it may be attractive as many states have competitive federal grants available for groups who wish to create charter schools in coed or single-gender formats.

CHAPTER 9 PLANNING TOOL: BUDGETING AND THE IMPACT OF GENDER

Use the chart below to list your current and projected budget. Then estimate the cost that may be incurred related to items that are specific to the single-gender program.

	Current	Projected	Gender Specific
Facilities			
Communication			
Teacher Allocation			
Teaching Materials			
Classroom Furniture			
Technology			
Textbooks			
Professional Development			
Transportation			
Enrichment			
Field Studies			

- Total student enrollment:

- Projected student enrollment in single-gender classes:

- Percent of total student population projected to be enrolled in single-gender classes:

- How does this information impact your budget considerations?

- Are there any grant opportunities available?

PART III

Implementing a Single-Gender Program

Many education reform efforts are brilliantly conceived but poorly implemented. Too often, teachers are left without support during the school year.

As illustrated in Part II, much planning is necessary to create a quality single-gender program. However, it is the teacher who must make learning successful for students. It is the teacher who is faced with a class of all girls or all boys every day. It is the teacher who needs support throughout the year. And, it is the administrator who must keep expectations high for the teacher and provide the opportunities for the teacher to be successful. Without the collaboration of teacher and administrator at a school, a single-gender program could dissolve into an unsuccessful fad.

> *If I had the chance to do it over again, I would get more training for my teachers before we started.*

—Principal reflecting on her single-gender program in November after starting the program in August

> *We were just thrown into it.*

—Teacher in a single-gender program

111

10

Professional Development

A key component of all the strategies and approaches we suggest, integral to the very notion of reflecting on gender, is that teachers should not have to do this work in isolation.

—*Gender and Urban Education* (Ginsberg et al., 2004, p. 59)

Many decisions about education come from the top, such as textbook adoption, grading policies, and lesson plan formats. But announcing a single-gender program at a school without the support from teachers already lined up will lead to a rocky implementation. Unfortunately, there are plenty of principals who inform teachers as they are preparing for summer break, or even a week before school starts, that they will be teaching some single-gender classes. Chapter 7 discussed the need to communicate with different groups—teachers being one of them. Early involvement of teachers is critical to the faculty and staff buying into the program, and this includes professional development before classes start.

Professional development need not cost a lot of money, but it will take time and energy, both precious resources for teachers. Because single-gender programs are highly visible programs, often misunderstood by parents and staff when first announced, and have legal considerations, teachers need several sustained opportunities for professional development.

Initially teachers will need an introduction to the idea of single-gender education. More than likely, they will want to know about recent research on gender differences and the impact these differences can have within their classrooms. Ultimately, teachers will want to know what procedures they can use to better teach boys and girls. Teachers may push for specific "boy" and "girl" strategies or lesson plans. One reinforces stereotypes and limits students when lessons, strategies, or procedures are suggested that are good for only boys or only girls. It is for this reason that teachers should meet to share, reflect, and evaluate lessons, strategies, and procedures that they are using in their single-gender classes.

A word of caution: Unlike other educational programs (i.e., differentiated instruction, learning by design, and reading strategies), public school single-gender education is relatively new and there are few resources and organizations to tap into, though a list is provided in Resource D. Consequently, it is the teachers at each site who need to become resources for each other, while the principal carves out time for training and collaboration. The teachers and principal, then, are the foundation of a successful single-gender program. Recognizing that time is rare within many schools, principals may need to get creative with finding time for teachers to meet. Here are some possibilities:

- Plan school or district professional development days with time dedicated to single-gender education (or innovative strategies in general with single gender being one of the subgroups).
- Schedule early release days where teachers can meet for one hour a month or quarter.
- Schedule late start days where teachers can meet for one hour a month or quarter before school starts.
- Have teachers meet at lunchtime, with the administrators arranging for supervision of the students with themselves or parent volunteers (maybe even provide lunch for the teachers!).
- Arrange for coverage of classes with several substitutes so that several teachers can meet together. The substitutes could rotate among different classes so several different groups of teachers could meet during the school day.
- Hold an assembly and give teachers time to meet during the assembly.
- Have teachers meet while their students are in related arts classes.

The suggestions in this list are ways to get ideas flowing in creative ways. The focus is on getting teachers together to discuss single-gender education practices, research, and student performance.

Professional development ideas are grouped into two broad categories: prior to implementation and after implementation. The ideas are recommendations. Different ideas will be more successful and feasible at different schools. Possible timelines are also included.

PROFESSIONAL DEVELOPMENT OPPORTUNITIES PRIOR TO IMPLEMENTATION

Continue to Support "Best Practices"

Single-gender education does not replace other programs or initiatives at a school. Nor does single-gender education eliminate the best practice that already exists within schools. Ideally, it provides a context for continuing these efforts and blends into ongoing programs. In addition, single-gender education is a form of differentiated instruction where teachers are meeting the needs of individual students. Carol Ann Tomlinson, author of books on differentiated instruction, recognizes that gender is one of the four categories of the student learning profile (2001).

Looking at gender as a part of student learning, and how gender may affect the implementation of other programs or strategies, is critical. Providing preliminary or continued professional development on differentiated instruction, problem-based learning, and inquiry-based learning will help teachers become comfortable with modifying lessons for the students in their classes. Good teaching involves responding to the strengths and weaknesses of the students in order to create the best learning environment and activities. If teachers are not comfortable with modifying and adjusting lessons, launching a single-gender program can make them uncomfortable. Principals may want to prepare teachers for a single-gender program by first having them work with differentiated instruction as a way of meeting the needs of individual students.

Cultivate a Collaborative Culture

There is limited outside support for single-gender teachers at this time. Support will need to come from their colleagues. Teachers will need to be comfortable with discussing their teaching with others and welcome the opportunity to share insights without fear of critique or judgment. Educator, consultant, and author John Gabriel (2005) suggests:

> What they [leaders] fail to realize is that an initial level of trust needs to be established. So don't rush this process. It is only when we are comfortable with our vulnerability, or no longer feel vulnerable, that we are more willing to work together. (p. 111)

Building a school culture where this type of support and collaboration exists is important for any school, especially one starting a single-gender program. Teachers will need to be open to using data to make decisions about instruction. Team-building exercises for teachers can help.

Local organizations that offer outdoor-based, team-building sessions provide rich experiences. Principals can also organize team-building opportunities in their own school using ideas from books on team building.

Most of these ideas do not require additional resources, and providing time for teachers to connect is vital. Team-building activities can take place at the beginning of faculty meetings and during professional development days before school starts or during the year. Again, Gabriel (2005) cautions:

> Administrators who state, "Because you are professionals, you'll be able to work together," or who believe that departments will be effective because they are expect to be, miss the point entirely. They either don't understand human nature or choose to ignore its shortcomings. Don't make that mistake. Just as some classes engage in team-building activities in the beginning of the year to foster community, it is essential that you implement team-building and trust-building activities. (p. 108)

Visit Schools With Single-Gender Programs

Nothing really convinces teachers about single-gender education more than actually seeing students working in single-gender classes. Visiting a school with single-gender classes is invaluable. The National Association for Single-Sex Public Education (www.nasspe.org) keeps a list of single-gender schools as well as schools with single-gender classes. The state of South Carolina Department of Education has an office for Single-Gender Initiatives and maintains a list of schools with single-gender classes (www.ed.sc.gov/sgi).

Get Connected With National Organizations

The 2006 federal regulations did not address how to best prepare teachers for single-gender classes. South Carolina is the only state that has created a position in its Department of Education to support districts, schools, and teachers as they consider and implement single-gender education. Other state agencies may follow.

There are national organizations that work with single-gender programs. Currently there are at least six organizations. This list is not a recommendation for any of the organizations, but a place for schools to start their research on supporting organizations. Each of these organizations holds a yearly conference on issues related to gender and education, and principals and teachers can attend these conferences to better understand the issues related to single-gender education as well as learn about others' experiences.

- Coalition of Schools Educating Boys of Color (www.coseboc.org)
- The Gurian Institute (www.gurianinstitute.com)
- International Boys' School Coalition (www.theibsc.org)
- National Association for Single-Sex Public Education (www.nasspe.org)
- National Coalition of Girls' Schools (www.ncgs.org)
- National Conference on Single-Sex Public Schools (www.ncssps.org)

Contact National Consultants

There are several consultants who travel the country giving presentations on gender differences and single-gender education. Doing an Internet search on "single-gender education," "single-sex education," "boys' education," or "girls' education" is a starting point for finding speakers. In addition, searching for authors of books on gender differences or books on strategies for working with boys and girls also provides options.

Not all consultants present the same information, and it is important to thoroughly review the speaker's qualifications concerning single-gender education. Some questions to guide your speaker research might include the following:

- What is the speaker's perspective on the performance issue of boys and girls and what does the speaker recommend as strategies to address these issues?
- How does the speaker suggest schools address the socialization issues of boys and girls?
- Does the speaker have ideas about working with hormonal differences between boys and girls?
- What is the speaker's view on brain-based differences between boys and girls and how should educators address these differences?
- Is the speaker an educator and what is his or her background?
- Is the speaker a professional in the field of psychology, biology, neurology, sociology, or other related field that relates to gender differences?
- Has the speaker taught within a single-gender classroom?
- Is the speaker a teacher?
- Is the speaker knowledgeable about the federal regulations and ongoing challenges?

There are a variety of views on these issues so it is important that an administrator have a clear understanding of the speaker's perspectives. Principals need to make sure that there is a match between the speaker and school's focus for single-gender education.

Conduct Book Studies

There are many texts regarding how boys and girls learn. Administrators could select one book for a faculty to read or provide a choice among several books. Organizing a book study takes planning and is beyond the focus of this book. However, with any book study, it is important to follow up after assigned reading takes place. Some useful questions focusing on gender for follow-up sessions are the following:

- What do you agree with and why?
- What do you disagree with and why?
- Which information surprised you?

- Did the author describe a child similar to one you teach? In what way? Is this important to you as a teacher?
- Can you think of a child of the same gender that does not follow that description? How does this information help you as a teacher?
- What are three ideas you can use in your classroom right now? After trying these three, what do you notice in your students?
- Does the book stereotype boys and girls? If so, in what way?
- Does the author cite sources for the claims made in the book? If so, are the sources reliable? If not, how does that affect the author's credibility?
- Does this book support your efforts with a single-gender program? In what way?
- What is the main idea that you want to pass on to others who have not read this book?

Conduct Focus Question Groups

Having groups of teachers work together on focus questions is valuable because it gives teachers a chance to address their concerns. Gabriel (2005) argues, "When there is no meaningful professional development, or teachers don't reflect on their practices, they stagnate or they stunt their own growth. Their zeal for the job dulls and they only go through the motions" (p. 114). Some schools use the "professional learning community" format for collaborative professional development. This is a structured format for engaging teachers in reflective teacher-based professional development.

The general idea is this: Teachers write a question or concern they want to explore concerning single-gender education. Each of these concerns is categorized into themes, such as boys, girls, stereotypes, self-confidence, academic achievement, advisory, classroom management, boy code, bullying, and relational aggression. Teachers choose a particular theme to explore using the questions listed. From that point, each group determines how it will proceed. Pedro Noguera (2008) argues that teacher collaboration must be central to professional development. He explains, "Every staff meeting focuses on professional development. Teachers share their expertise and material, and they discuss ways to ensure they reach all students. They discuss how to align instructional strategies to the curriculum and state-mandated assessments in creative, compelling ways" (p. 165).

Research can involve reading texts and conducting student and teacher surveys, classroom observations, and Internet searches. It is important to have periodic opportunities to discuss findings. While a focus group may have their own questions or format for discussion, Alice Ginsberg and her colleagues (2004) offer these to consider:

- How does the research conducted, sample used, and conclusions drawn compare with what I've observed in my own classroom or school?
- In what ways did the research confirm my own beliefs/assumptions/observations, and in what ways did it dispute them?

- How satisfactorily do I think the research answered the questions it set out to address?
- What questions are still unanswered?
- What additional questions does the research raise for me?
- What questions do I want to pursue further?
- As a result of this research, how will I look at my classroom or school differently? (p. 54)

In the end, each group presents its discoveries to the staff. This can be done in a formal presentation to the whole faculty, in rotations of small-group discussions, or in a fair format, where posters are arranged around a room.

Collaborate With Colleges and Universities

Colleges and universities do not offer certificates in single-gender education at this time; however, higher-education departments are becoming more aware of the issue. Some local professors may be well versed in the issue of single gender and be willing to serve as a resource for the district or school. They might have a lecture to present to the faculty, and there are some colleges that offer courses in gender differences or single-gender education. More specifically, the South Carolina Department of Education created an online recertification course available to all South Carolina teachers. Similar online opportunities may be available through other state institutions, colleges, or universities.

POSSIBLE TIMELINES TO PREPARE TEACHERS PRIOR TO IMPLEMENTATION

Here, three typical timeframes are offered in which single-gender programs take root. The ideas listed are minimal suggestions and the ones that are the most cost-effective. The lists vary based upon the amount of time that is available for teachers to dedicate to each activity. Certainly, hiring a consultant to work with staff is beneficial, but it can also be costly.

One Year to Prepare Teachers

Having at least one year to prepare allows teachers to explore concerns they have regarding gender differences and single-gender education. It also provides time for teachers to become comfortable with the idea of meeting the needs of individual students. Suggestions for this timeframe include the following:

- Form focus groups.
- Visit schools with single-gender programs or attend a national conference.
- Try some single-gender strategies in the classroom.
- Analyze school data by subgroups (i.e., gender and ethnicity) and discuss how a single-gender program could benefit students and the school.
- Introduce and reinforce differentiated instruction.
- Conduct a book study.

Six Months to Prepare Teachers

Six months is a common timeframe for teachers to prepare for single-gender classes. Typically, schools begin looking at changes for the following school year in January. Suggestions for this timeframe include the following:

- Conduct a book study.
- Visit schools with single-gender programs.
- Attend training or a national conference and present findings to staff.
- Hold sessions on how a single-gender program will benefit students and the school.

Three Months to Prepare Teachers

Three months can be too short to adequately prepare teachers, but it is not impossible. Teachers might feel they are tossed into single-gender classes without a clear understanding as to why the program exists and what they are expected to do. Suggestions for this timeframe include the following:

- Hire a consultant to train teachers.
- Distribute news articles to teachers regarding single-gender programs so they know that other schools are involved in this process.
- Provide Web sites for teachers to explore on their own, with a structure for sharing findings.
- Provide texts for teachers to read as time permits with central questions pertinent to your school.

CONTINUED PROFESSIONAL DEVELOPMENT AFTER IMPLEMENTATION

Teacher training doesn't end after the program begins. Each point listed as an idea prior to implementation can begin or continue after the program is implemented. Some principals decide to hire consultants after the program is up and running so teachers have some context in which to ask questions. Other principals have teachers refine or continue focus-group discussions. But there are other ways to improve teaching in single-gender classes.

Create Lesson Plans

Lessons for boys and girls don't have to be different, but there may be different methods for direct instruction or group work. Also, using different examples or emphasizing different parts of the text might work better with boys or girls. Listing these differences within lesson plans makes planning for boys and girls a conscious process. It also provides an opportunity for teachers to reflect on the impact these strategies have on girls and boys. Through collaboration, this process helps a school develop its own set of teaching methods for a single-gender format. Furthermore, successful ideas can be shared with all teachers.

Listing strategies in lesson plans also provides a focus for classroom observations. Upon visiting classes, administrators are able to see what was planned, what is happening in the classroom, and then are able to make suggestions. This process can ensure that there is equity in learning experiences for boys and girls.

Having teachers commit to trying three to five strategies per unit provides a structure for teacher expectations and context for teacher discussions. Furthermore, teachers of boys and teachers of girls can discuss which strategies they want to commit to trying as a group to ensure consistency across the program. During this discussion, teachers should explain why they want to use certain strategies with boys and with girls. Consequently, biases and stereotypes will surface and can be addressed, as well as teachers' understanding of gender differences. Over the course of the year, additional strategies can be added and others removed. In the end, there will be a solid ground upon which the program can grow.

Provide Time for Team Planning,
Sharing, or Focus-Group Discussions

Teachers in the single-gender program should have time to come together and share experiences and strategies. Ideally, this meeting time is a part of their regular meeting schedule and not an additional meeting before or after school. This meeting time could be the regularly scheduled meeting on curriculum or the time for team, grade-level, or content-area planning. It is possible that a different meeting rotation will need to be put into place in order to accommodate the different meetings that need to take place. Weekly, or at least monthly, teachers should share three strategies that they implemented successfully and how students responded. Teachers should also share three strategies that were not successful. The other teachers can provide ideas or ask probing questions to help the presenting teachers refine their practice. Some schools also use this time to continue their professional learning community or focus-group discussions.

Present at National, State, or Local Conferences on Subject Areas or Grade Levels

There are national, state, and local conferences for different subjects, such as mathematics, language arts, science, and social studies. Recently, teachers have presented their experiences with single-gender classes at these conferences. Encouraging and supporting teachers to present what they do in the classroom can strengthen a teacher's practice. Presenting at these conferences also provides a chance to develop a network of other interested educators.

Host a Local, State, or Regional Conference

Your own school can open its doors to educators interested in single-gender education. The TWO Academies at Dent Middle School in Columbia, South Carolina, hosted a Saturday conference on strategies for boys and girls. Educators from across the Southeast (as well as two from the Northeast) attended. Kingstree Junior High in Kingstree, South Carolina, had forty educators from around the state visit its single-gender classes on one Wednesday and interact with different panels of its teachers.

Reflect on Data

All teachers should review their data and do so by different subgroups, such as gender, race, and socioeconomic status. Who is passing and who is failing? Who disrupts the class and who is not participating? Who is challenging themselves and who is just getting by? By implementing a single-gender program, a school commits itself to examine data by gender. Teachers can look at their own data with each unit, and the school can review data each quarter or marking period.

TIMELINE TO SUPPORT TEACHERS AFTER IMPLEMENTATION

First Year of Implementation

During the first quarter or marking period:

- Develop lesson plans with strategies or procedures for boys and girls and discuss.

During the second quarter or marking period:

- Develop lesson plans with strategies or procedures for boys and girls and discuss.
- Analyze and reflect on data.

During the third quarter or marking period:

- Develop lesson plans with strategies or procedures for boys and girls and discuss.
- Analyze and reflect on data.
- Conduct teacher focus groups.

During the fourth quarter or marking period:

- Develop lesson plans with strategies or procedures for boys and girls and discuss.
- Analyze and reflect on data.
- Conduct teacher focus groups.

Second Year of Implementation

- Develop lesson plans with strategies or procedures for boys and girls and discuss.
- Analyze and reflect on data.
- Conduct teacher focus groups.
- Present at national, state, or local conferences on content area or grade level.
- Attend or present at national, state, or local conferences related to single-gender education.

Third Year of Implementation

- Develop lesson plans with strategies or procedures for boys and girls and discuss.
- Analyze and reflect on data.
- Conduct teacher focus groups.
- Present at national, state, or local conferences on content area or grade level.
- Attend or present at national, state, or local conferences related to single-gender education.
- Host a single-gender conference or workshop at your school for local, state, or national educators.

CHAPTER 10 PLANNING TOOL: DEVELOPING A PROFESSIONAL DEVELOPMENT PLAN

Use the following prompts to help plan professional development. Teachers will be more comfortable about what is expected and know that they have support from the administration. Parents will see a plan for success. The district office will be aware of your needs.

Plan Prior to Implementation

- What budget do you have available?

- What ways can you create or continue a culture of collaboration?

- What best practices do you want to have continued at your school?

- What are your priorities for supporting teachers?

Professional Development Activity	Expected Outcome	Materials Needed and Cost	Person Responsible for Arranging Activity	Timeframe for Activity

Plan After Implementation

- What budget do you have available?
- What are your expectations for the use of and reflection on strategies for boys and girls?
- What are your priorities for supporting teachers?

Professional Development Activity	Expected Outcome	Materials Needed and Cost	Person Responsible for Arranging Activity	Timeframe for Activity

11

Program Evaluation

The federal regulations require that public school single-gender programs review their program at least every two years to ensure that they are not discriminating and are meeting their own rationale. Hopefully, schools will review their data more often, at least yearly if not quarterly.

Before a school implements a single-gender program, it is good to have a structure in place to gather the necessary data. The following information can serve as a starting point or guide to assist principals as they create their own program evaluation formats.

ENSURING NONDISCRIMINATION

There are four areas that create opportunities for discrimination in a single-gender format: program structure, facilities, curriculum, and instruction. Certainly, if staff members specifically tell students that they cannot participate because of their sex, then that could be grounds for discrimination and would need to be investigated. Yet, that can happen in any situation and is not necessarily a single-gender issue.

Program Structure

The overall structure of the single-gender program should be the same for boys and girls, which means the same classes need to be offered to boys and girls. The classes need to be the same length of time. The same data-reflection process needs to be used for boys and girls. Academic and discipline data should be examined by gender, and the results should speak for themselves. Administrators shouldn't just look at academic data for boys and discipline data for girls or vice versa. Providing information to parents should be the same. Letters can't be sent to the parents of boys, and an informational meeting held for parents of girls. The lesson planning process and teacher meeting time should be the same for teachers of girls and teachers of boys. And, the same process of data collection to review the program needs to be used for classes of boys and classes of girls. We would not want to gather standardized test scores for boys and class averages for girls.

These issues apply to all of the teachers in the school. However, given that single-gender programs are under scrutiny, it is important to make sure these issues take place in a nondiscriminatory manner.

Facilities

The physical layout of the boy classes and girl classes, as well as the actual classrooms, need to be "substantially equal." The hallways, classrooms, desks, and tables need to be "substantially equal." They don't have to be identical, but "substantially equal" qualities include age, damage, and usability. Details including quality of carpet; quality of paint; room size; and classroom furniture, such as bookcases, shelves, and couches, need be examined to ensure "substantially equal" status. Certainly, teacher preference and budgets come into play when classrooms are maintained; however, the reason for differences cannot be because it is a girls' room or a boys' room. The cleanliness of the halls, bathrooms, and classrooms should be "substantially equal" as well.

There has been some controversy over painting the walls of girl classes and boy classes. Selecting the color of the walls with gender in mind could lead to stereotyping of students. Caution should be taken if a school is considering this step.

An important area of facility comparison is technology. The quality and quantity of technology needs to be similar. Overhead projectors, interactive whiteboards, and computers should be distributed equally among girl and boy classes.

Curriculum

The same state or district standards must be taught in single-gender and coed classes. Teachers cannot ignore or change the curriculum because they teach a group of girls or a group of boys. If the school has one group of teachers teaching boys and another group teaching girls at the same grade level, then these teachers should meet by grade level for planning and pacing. If a school is departmentalized and has one group of teachers teaching boys and another group teaching girls, then these teachers should meet by content area for planning and pacing. Documentation of these meetings and copies of lesson plans showing the same standards or topics being taught are evidence of nondiscrimination in curriculum.

Instruction

Showing nondiscrimination in regards to instruction can be difficult because different teachers teach lessons differently. Teachers respond to the group of students whom they are teaching at that time based on their pace of understanding, questions they pose, and level of prior understanding.

The key remedy is to provide "substantially equal" learning opportunities for girls and boys. This involves making sure teachers of boys and girls both provide access to higher-order thinking opportunities, hands-on activities, and engaging activities. Teachers need to be aware of the level of questioning for their girls and boys. Do they both get recall questions as well as comparison and evaluative questions? Are boys and girls provided opportunities to learn through math manipulatives, hands-on activities and projects? Are girls and boys engaged in role-playing scenes from the text, acting out vocabulary words, and learning through movement?

Some teachers read books or hear speakers talk about boys' need for movement and girls' use of color. On the surface, this could seem to be stereotyping. However, teachers see that this information benefits instruction in the classroom as well as aids learning for students, and then they can incorporate these ideas into their teaching. The danger is in interpreting the information as meaning that only boys need to move and only girls enjoy color and not giving students opportunities.

In terms of program evaluation, a teacher can use the information about movement and color and provide opportunities for both boys and girls. The teacher can come up with movement activities with the boys in mind, but then use some of those activities with the girls. Color can be used to engage girls in a project, but make color available to the boys as well. Remember there is great variety within each sex as well, so multiple learning opportunities are necessary for boys and girls.

Allowing students to make choices about their learning activities can aid in being nondiscriminatory. Choices involve a variety of activities based on student learning style, multiple intelligences, student interest, gendered information, and district and school expectations.

REVIEWING THE RATIONALE: FORMAT

In addition to academic achievement, improving student behavior and attendance are often included as goals for single-gender programs.

When looking at the data, critics of single-gender programs will rightly ask, "How do we know that the single-gender program is the cause of the difference?" The simple answer is that we don't know. Single-gender programs are completely voluntary, and this creates a variable that cannot be controlled. A parent's interest in single-gender classes can be a determining factor in a child's performance. Ongoing math, reading, or science programs at the school could also be a factor. A whole-school behavior program is a factor as well, along with interaction among teachers.

Given the variety of factors and expense of formal studies, schools face the difficult task of ascertaining the impact of a single-gender program. In order to understand the impact of single-gender classes, data from single-gender classes should be compared to some other type of data. It is commendable if all the students pass a class, score proficient on a standardized test, or have no discipline referrals. However, is that typical for these students, this grade level, or this school? Did single gender actually help make that happen? There are three ways to compare these data.

Students in Single-Gender Classes
Compared to Students in Coed Classes

One of the most obvious ways to look at data is to compare students in single-gender classes to students in coed classes. Yet, principals should consider the potential negative impact this form of comparison can have on staff morale. By comparing the single-gender classes to coed classes, the teachers might see themselves in competition. In some cases, the teachers of the coed classes may feel they need to have their students perform worse so that the students in single-gender classes can shine. This comes from the idea that single gender is a new initiative with substantial time and energy invested in its success.

Table 11.1 shows a way to compare students who are currently enrolled in single-gender classes with students who are currently enrolled in coed classes. It is important that the classes have similar demographics and previous performance. The data can be sorted by coed classes and single-gender classes, but then also sorted by gender in each of the areas (coed and single gender). This double breakdown allows the school community to determine if boys or girls are impacted more, less, or at the same level by single-gender classes. Data can be sorted by individual students in specific classes, class averages based on the teacher's class roster, averages based on subject area, or averages based on grade level.

Students in Single-Gender Classes Compared
to Previous Performance in Coed Classes

A different, and possibly more difficult, format compares students against their own previous performance. This is difficult because data are not the same year to year, especially if students change schools. Further, there is no way to control for the variables that affect a child's achievement.

Table 11.1   Comparison Format for Coed and Single-Gender Data

	(Choose One) Standardized Test Scores Class Grade Point Averages Discipline Referrals Attendance							
	2009–2010 Coed				2009–2010 Single Gender			
	Female		Male		Female		Male	
	#	%	#	%	#	%	#	%
(Choose One)								
Student								
Teacher's Class Subject Area								
Grade Level								

However, the benefit of looking at students' own growth is that it focuses on the actual students being taught and doesn't create competition among teachers of single-gender classes and coed classes.

Table 11.2 (pages 130–131) shows a way to organize student data from year to year. Individual students would be listed by gender, and the selected data would be posted in each column.

Students in Single-Gender Classes Compared to Averages of Previous Students in Coed Classes

It is possible to compare students in single-gender classes with students in coed classes without causing negative feedback from teachers by gathering averages of data for several years in which students were in coed classes and then comparing that average against data from students enrolled in single-gender classes. There are short-comings with this approach, though, which include studying different students, different years, and other different programs that existed at the school. However, if there seems to be consistency in performance by students in subject areas or a consistent level of discipline referrals across several years, then this format provides insight. Administrators should already have the averages from when the rationale was created. Table 11.3 (page 133) shows a way to organize a comparison of averages from previous years.

Table 11.2 Comparison Format for Individual Students

	2008–2009 Coed Classes								2009–2010 Single-Gender Classes							
	1.	2.	3.	4.	5.	6.	7.	8.	1.	2.	3.	4.	5.	6.	7.	8.
Females																
Female Student A (Name or Student Number)																
Female Student B (Name or Student Number)																
(Continue With Female Students C, D, E, etc.)																
Males																
Male Student A (Name or Student Number)																
Male Student B (Name or Student Number)																

	2008–2009 Coed Classes								2009–2010 Single-Gender Classes							
	1.	2.	3.	4.	5.	6.	7.	8.	1.	2.	3.	4.	5.	6.	7.	8.
Males																
(Continue With Male Students C, D, E, etc.)																
Average for Females																
Average for Males																

Column Coding (selected data):

1. ELA grade.

2. Math grade.

3. Science grade.

4. Social studies grade.

5. Discipline referrals.

6. Attendance.

7. Standardized test score for ELA.

8. Standardized test score for math.

Table 11.3   Several-Year Comparison Format for Coed and Single-Gender Averages

	Average During 2006–2007, 2007–2008, 2008–2009: Coed Classes		Average During 2009–2010: Single-Gender Classes		Difference	
	Female	*Male*	*Female*	*Male*	*Female*	*Male*
ELA Class Average						
Math Class Average						
Science Class Average						
Standardized Test Score Average—ELA						
Standardized Test Score Average—Math						
Standardized Test Score Average—Science						
Discipline Referral Average						
Average Attendance						

Averages for the three years do not need to be used; class averages for each individual year can be compared to the performance during the year of single-gender classes. Table 11.4 is an example of this format.

REVIEWING THE DATA: INDICATORS

The rationale of a single-gender program identifies a goal for the students in the program. In many cases, the rationale is a general statement about increasing or decreasing a student category, such as performance, behavior, or attitude. Within each category, specific indicators can be used as data. Determining which indicator to use can be based on the needs of the

Table 11.4 One-Year Comparison Format for Coed and Single-Gender Averages

	Average During 2007–2008 Coed Classes		Average During 2008–2009 Coed Classes		Average During 2009–2010 Single-Gender Classes	
	Female	*Male*	*Female*	*Male*	*Female*	*Male*
ELA Class Average						
Math Class Average						
Science Class Average						
Standardized Test Score Average—ELA						
Standardized Test Score Average—Math						
Standardized Test Score Average—Science						
Discipline Referral Average						
Average Attendance						

school, the specific intent of the program, and ease of gathering the data. The ideas below are suggestions and not meant to be an exhaustive list or intended to all be included within a program evaluation.

Indicators of increased academic performance:

- Baseline standardized test scores
- Percentage or number of students scoring at each level (below basic, basic, proficient, advanced)
- Percentage or number of students with classroom grades at each level
- Averages of classroom grades
- Percentage or number of students passing with a C or above
- Percentage or number of students meeting target growth

- Percentage or number of students exceeding target growth
- Student survey on self-confidence, desire to succeed, participation, trying new tasks, academic risk taking, or goal setting

Indicators of decreased retention rate:

- Percentage or number of students passing a course
- Percentage or number of students passing end-of-course test
- Percentage or number of students retained
- Student survey on self-confidence, self-esteem, goal setting, determination

Indicators of decreased drop-out rate:

- Percentage or number of students dropping out
- Percentage or number of students retained
- Student survey on self-confidence, self-esteem, goal setting, determination

Indicators of improved student behavior and/or decreased discipline referrals:

- Percentage or number of student referrals
- Teacher survey on behavior, distractions, focus, participation, engagement
- Student survey on behavior, distractions, focus, participation, engagement
- Classroom observations
- Analysis of videotape of classroom instruction

Indicators of increased student self-concept:

- Student survey on self-confidence, self-esteem, goal setting, determination
- Parent survey on self-confidence, self-esteem, goal setting, determination of child
- Focused interviews with students
- Focused interviews with parents

Indicators of improved student attitude:

- Student survey on self-confidence, self-esteem, goal setting, determination
- Parent survey on self-confidence, self-esteem, goal setting, determination of child
- Focused interviews with students
- Focused interviews with parents
- Percentage or number of students enrolling in specific courses (e.g., higher-level science, math, computer science, etc.)

AN ONGOING REVIEW PROCESS

Reviewing a single-gender program is ongoing. Although federal regulations require a program be reviewed every two years, more frequent reassessment improves student learning and the effectiveness of the program. Weekly classroom observations and review of lesson plans, as well as time for teacher reflection, are opportunities for professional development. The review process and program evaluation are informative rather than punitive, and gathering data on a quarterly or semester basis helps teachers gauge whether their practices have an impact on students. Ideas for professional development are discussed in Chapter 10.

CHAPTER 11 PLANNING TOOL: PREPARING FOR EVALUATION

- Brainstorm ways to evaluate your program:

- State the rationale for your program:

- List the data that you used to create your rationale:

- What format will you use to ensure nondiscrimination . . .
  In your program structure?
  In your facility?
  In the curriculum?
  In teacher instruction?

- What format will you use for reviewing the program rationale?
  Comparison to current coed classes:
  Comparison to previous performance of same students:
  Comparison to previous averages of coed classes:
  Other:

- What indicators have you selected to review the rationale?
  Academic:
  Behavioral:
  Attitudinal:
  Other:

- Who is the person to be responsible for gathering data?

- What is the deadline for having baseline data?

- What is the deadline for having data for the current year of the program?

12

Sustaining a Single-Gender Program

And any environment is a chance environment so far as its educative influence is concerned unless it has been deliberately regulated with reference to its educative effect.

—John Dewey, *Democracy and Education*

Perhaps the most difficult part of starting any program is keeping momentum going. The daily pressures and demands of teaching often crowd out attention needed to nurture a new program. Single-gender programs are no different. Time should be dedicated to monitoring the program, but balance is needed so every meeting isn't dominated by gender issues and teachers don't go numb with overload. This chapter will offer ways to sustain the successful implementation of a single-gender program. Every idea won't be useful for every school, so schools should consider which ideas are important for their unique community and create a probable timeline.

STRONG PRINCIPAL LEADERSHIP

The most important factor for getting a program going is the leadership of the principal. If the principal provides time and resources to the program, keeping it a top priority, the program likely will be successful. If the principal agrees to the program only because of teacher or district pressure, makes numerous demands on the teachers in addition to teaching a single-gender class, and doesn't provide planning time for teachers, then the program will have difficulty getting off the ground and making it to the second year.

Robert Marzano and his colleagues (2005) studied successful school leadership, especially leadership that involves "deep and dramatic change." The authors do not specifically cite implementing single-gender programs; however, we can safely assume that changing the structure of the classroom from coed to single-gender is "deep and dramatic change." They conclude there are seven factors relevant to leadership during deep change:

1. Knowledge of curriculum, instruction and assessment: The principal (or team leader) needs to stay abreast of single-gender education and how it will impact curriculum. Attending conferences or workshops, communicating with other administrators involved with single-gender education, and review of current texts is important.

2. Optimizer: The principal has to be supportive of the change or others will not rally to the cause.

3. Intellectual Stimulation: One way to be supportive is to keep information about single-gender education and gender differences in front of the faculty. This can include news articles about other single-gender programs across the country, quotes from relevant texts related to gender differences, and texts that discuss the issue of gender. Conducting quick Internet searches on "single-gender education," "single-sex education," and "gender differences" will provide plenty of resources. Using Internet alerts on these topics can deliver automatic daily digests that can then be circulated to staff members or posted during faculty meetings. Articles and texts can be presented as a way to open debate and discussion.

4. Change Agent: Single-gender education is a change from the traditional coed classroom. As a change agent, the principal will need to continually remind the faculty about the rationale for the single-gender program, what it can do for the school and students, and the data that were used to support the decision.

5. Monitoring/Evaluating: As required by the federal regulations, the program has to be reviewed every two years, but more frequent monitoring is helpful for teacher feedback.

6. Flexibility: Listening to teachers, students, and parents could lead to changes in the original format of the program. It is important to be flexible to how the program is implemented, but to be consistent with its purpose.

7. Ideas/Beliefs: Remember the reasons for creating the program and its goal.

A new program should have short-term and long-term goals. In the short-term, the staff monitors the impact of the program and discusses what happens in their classrooms. The principal should allow a three- to five-year transition period. The first year is new, and parents, students, and teachers will be figuring out what kind of program they want at the school. Initial data can be collected, and changes made to schedules, policies, and teacher assignments. During this year, teachers will become more comfortable with teaching all boys or all girls. The second year provides an opportunity to thoroughly examine instructional practices, program design, and the impact single-gender classes are having on students. The third year allows for continued data collection, and some patterns may emerge. During the fourth and fifth years, educators establish the program as an integral part of the school.

INSTITUTIONALIZE THE SINGLE-GENDER PROGRAM

One of most frequent causes for a single-gender program to be abandoned is staff turnover. One year, there might be five teachers who are passionate about the program, but three leave for a variety of reasons. The other two can't garner enough support for the program, and it dies. The same is true if a principal leaves. This is unfortunate, as it sends a message to the staff and the community that any new program will be gone as soon as the point person leaves. Consequently, the time and effort to institutionalize a single-gender program by reviewing data, writing a rationale, and communicating with the community are important investments.

Communication

There are small, but powerful, actions to institutionalize the single-gender program into a school through communication with the community. The idea is to make the program a visible and integral part of the whole school. It is also important to continually communicate what the program is and the benefits that students are receiving. The following list illustrates the actions a school can take to institutionalize the program.

1. List the program in the school newsletter as part of the school's array of educational choices. The listing should contain a short explanation of the program and something positive about it. With each issue, something new is mentioned.

2. List the program and its rationale on the school Web site. The district could also list the single-gender program on the district Web site and provide a link to the school site. Downplaying the single-gender program could make the public suspicious.

3. Include the program on the school's fax cover sheet. The fax cover sheet can announce the achievements of all programs—athletic and

academic—at the school. This will be a consistent reminder to the public about the great things going on at the school.

4.   Hold a question-and-answer session periodically for parents. Some schools hold "Muffins with Moms" or "Doughnuts with Dads" to develop relationships with parents. Keeping the lines of communication open is important for single-gender programs. These steps make the program visible and integral to the school, which is important in the eyes of the community.

Staff Meetings

To build support among the faculty, the principal or team leader should regularly explain how the single-gender program fits with the school's mission and isn't just a quick fix to increase student test scores. Often this is done during staff meetings or email updates. Also, it is important to include all staff members in professional development opportunities related to gender in order to build cohesion. Teachers of coed classes have insights into teaching boys and girls as well.

Lesson Plans

Requiring teachers to complete lesson plans that highlight how they work with boys and girls keeps the issue of gender in the foreground. While this makes sense for teachers of single-gender classes, the school should address gender needs across the whole school. The principal could require all teachers to document efforts they are making to better meet the needs of girls and boys, ensure equity, and address stereotyping. Administrators should ask reflective questions about a teacher's lesson, such as How did the lesson go? I noticed this is the first time you tried this strategy—was that comfortable for you? Did it make a difference with your students? Do you think you should try a different approach next time? How could a video clip engage your boys or girls? These questions are meant to be open-ended and support teachers as they reflect on their lessons. Faculty meetings could begin with small-group discussions or gallery walks highlighting creative ideas from teachers.

Teacher Meetings

Most schools have a weekly schedule for meetings during or after school. Grade-level meetings, faculty meetings, team meetings, and subject-area meetings are all planned in advance. Often they occur on the same day, rotating week by week. In addition to full-faculty meetings when the entire staff looks at gender issues, the principal should include a meeting time for all teachers of single-gender classes to discuss strategies and concerns as well as celebrate student successes. Teachers need the support of others who are in similar situations. Just as math teachers, cocurricular teachers, or second-grade teachers need to discuss what is happening in their classes, teachers of single-gender classes need to meet with each other. If at all possible, teachers should be given opportunities to observe each other's classroom as well as visit other schools with single-gender programs.

KEEP THE PROGRAM MANAGEABLE

Other reasons single-gender programs fall apart are scheduling conflicts and increased tension with the new schedule. In the beginning, teachers and principals see single gender as a wonderful opportunity and viable option. Parent satisfaction is high, and student performance is increasing. Given this situation, the principal then expands the single-gender program across the school. In some cases, this works. In others, it stretches the master schedule and overburdens teachers. Before expanding the program, the school should review data, reflect on the rationale for the program, and get feedback from parents, students, and teachers. Remember, single-gender education must be offered as a choice, not a mandate. If a school community wants to expand its program to incorporate more grades or more classes (even the whole school), then the district should consider designating the whole school as a single gender and another school as coed. Parts II and III of this book address this transition.

AGREE ON STRATEGIES TO USE WITH BOYS AND GIRLS

Teachers often request training on how to teach boys and girls. They want strategies, but this is a delicate issue. One the one hand, a class of boys could respond differently to certain activities than a class of girls, and to be effective, teachers need to know how to anticipate and work with this. On the other hand, the possibility of stereotyping is there whenever a teacher talks about what might work for girls and for boys as a group. Furthermore, it isn't the strategy that differs and most impacts the success, but the procedures used to implement strategies. The teacher may model a skill for classes of boys and girls, but the way it is modeled may be different. Or, a discussion is planned for the classes, but how the discussion proceeds might be different. Finally, there is nothing that both boys and girls can't accomplish in school; but, different procedures can be used to allow boy and girls to achieve those accomplishments. However, most teachers talk in terms of strategies.

As a group, single-gender teachers should agree on five to ten strategies to use with the girls and the boys and commit to trying these strategies over the course of a month, keeping a record of responses they get from students. The strategies can be the same for boys and girls, can include some similar strategies, or be completely different. Coming to consensus on these strategies involves teachers explaining why a strategy is important enough to make the list, which allows for discussion of possible stereotyping. In the end, teachers will go into their classrooms with a clear understanding of what is expected and methods to document how well the strategies work for their students. A process for agreeing on these strategies is highlighted at the end of this section (Table 12.1).

Teachers may not have time to come to agreement on strategies. The process could also be uncomfortable for some teachers if they are not accustomed to reflecting on their practice. It is important to consider the following insight by educator Doug Reeves (2006). He says real school improvement comes from three distinct factors: "While planning documents may be requirements mandated by federal, state, and local authorities, they are insufficient to improve student achievement and educational equity. As the evidence will show, it's all about monitoring, implementing, and execution" (p. 65). Only by committing to specific practices can teachers begin to monitor what works for *their* students.

Determining the Top Ten Procedures or Strategies for a School

Creating a compiled list can be accomplished in many ways. One successful way is described here.

- Teachers individually brainstorm a list of strategies they believe are important to use in classes. These can be gender-based procedures, general practices of good teaching, or district mandates.

- Teachers meet in small groups by teams, content area, or grade level to discuss and refine the list. Teachers have to justify why a strategy is being listed for boys or girls. A larger, combined list is then compiled. Additional small-group meetings can occur.

- Teachers of single-gender classes combine their lists. Strategies can be further categorized and refined. A professional discussion can take place in order to clarify the reasons for a strategy to be on the list or in a category. Questions can be answered.

- A consensus can be developed over a period of time through discussion, use of examples, and collaboration. Teachers can also vote on which ones belong on the top ten list, with each teacher voting for ten strategies for boys and girls. The ten strategies with the most votes end up on the final list. Teachers can also be given ten votes and distribute those votes in any way they see fit. For example, teachers may split their ten votes between two strategies by giving five votes each or seven votes for one and three votes for another. Another teacher may decide to put all ten votes on one procedure or strategy. The ten strategies with the most votes make the final list.

- The final list includes strategies that are comfortable for some teachers but cause others to stretch. It should not be expected that all procedures and strategies will be used in every lesson but implemented over the course of the month. They are also a minimum, not a limit, on what teachers can use.

Table 12.1   Sample Procedures for Boys and Girls

Procedures (Strategies) Often Used With Boys and Girls	
The goal of using a specific strategy is to engage students in learning. Different procedures are often used with groups of all boys and all girls (as well as within coed classes to increase engagement accordingly). However, the different strategies should never be used exclusively with one gender. All teachers should use strategies that best meet the needs of their own students. Further, strategies are meant as means to an end—part of the learning process that engages students. As students' skills improve, strategies should change accordingly.	
Sample Procedures Tending to Work With Boys *(This does not mean they aren't good with girls!)*	*Sample Procedures Tending to Work With Girls* *(This does not mean they aren't good with boys!)*
Have boys complete tasks in short chunks of time and use a timer that counts down and that students can see. If there are longer tasks, break them into smaller parts so that they can be specifically assigned and timed.	Create opportunities for discussions in different groupings: pairs, small group, and whole class. Discussions can center on student questions, teacher questions, inquiry opportunities, or making connections with the content.
Use a soft squish ball when boys are discussing a topic or the teacher is asking questions. The students can only talk when they have the ball and no intercepts are allowed. Ask the question, identify the student, and throw the ball.	Select the groups for the students in advance of the class and rotate seat assignments often. Deciding on groups during class can create an opportunity for girls to bully each other through comments of wanting to change groups.
Allow the boys to stand when taking notes, reading, working, or asking or answering questions. There can be a place in the room where students can stand if needed. Clipboards can be provided at that location.	Encourage girls to ask questions about content, take chances with their ideas, and try solutions before asking for teacher assistance or demonstration. However, try to respond to a question from a girl with a question to help her clarify what she needs and discover that she can accomplish the task. Limit the procedural questions.
Use a short and clear verbal cue to get the attention of boys before transitioning to a new activity or giving additional directions. Boys should have to respond verbally and physically to the verbal cue.	Incorporate role-playing as a way for girls to demonstrate their knowledge of the subject and extend their learning.

Require that boys predict their grades before turning in tests and projects. Have them provide a reason for their prediction, and use rubrics for projects. Once they receive their final grade, have them reflect on why there is a difference, if there is one.	Make a variety of colored materials available (pens, pencils, markers, overhead pens, paper). Allow their use with note-taking and projects, but do not emphasize the use of color over content or allow girls to spend more time on decorating than quality content.

MENTOR NEW TEACHERS

As a single-gender program progresses, a mentoring program can be implemented for new teachers. The program rationale and structure should be explained as well as the expectations for lessons, strategies, and collaborative planning. Teachers new to single-gender classes should receive some professional development either from within the school or district or from outside consultants.

New teachers should observe experienced teachers in their single-gender classes and then meet to discuss observations. Experienced teachers can then observe the new teachers. This would not be formal evaluation observations, but learning opportunities. Questions can be asked and suggestions provided. The school could incorporate this into any ongoing peer-observation process. Of course, this process of observation is beneficial for teachers involved in single-gender classes as well as coed classes.

CONTINUE PROFESSIONAL DEVELOPMENT

Faculty Professional Development

There are several opportunities for professional development after a program begins, as outlined in Chapter 10. Doug Reeves (2006) reminds us about the importance of providing professional development:

> The research suggests that when professional development efforts are focused on a few key elements, such as improving classroom feedback, assessment practices, and cross-disciplinary nonfiction writing, the yield in student achievement is significantly greater than when professional developers yield to the "flavor of the month" approach in which fads replace effectiveness. (p. 79)

Single-gender education can certainly become the next education fad if teachers do not continue to receive support. As suggested, professional development should center on a few items that allow for teachers to expand their knowledge, reflect on their practice, and analyze the performance of their students. Professional development need not center on gender differences, but schoolwide efforts could include writing across the curriculum or differentiated instruction, and be analyzed in terms of how the boys and girls are responding to the same lessons within the single-gender classes and the coed classes. This type of professional development discussion keeps gender on the agenda for the whole school and allows for rich dialogue among all teachers. Remember that the issue of gender should not replace other discussions about learning styles, race, poverty, ethnicity, or culture. Rather, gender is included as one of the points of reference to better understand the impact of teaching on student learning.

Individual Teacher Reflection

The idea of teacher reflection as a form of professional development is not new. Including gender and the way that boys and girls respond was done in light of gender-equity issues. Here, the suggestion is for teachers to answer their own questions about what works for boys and girls rather than hire consultants who talk about abstract theories and generalized research. Not only is this more cost-effective for schools, it is also more empowering for teachers.

Reeves (2006) developed a powerful format for teacher and principal reflection called a "leadership map." Using this leadership map, teachers can gauge the impact of different practices on student achievement. The Y-axis plots student achievement, such as percent of students scoring an A, B, or C on a unit test; reaching target growth on benchmark tests; turning in homework on time and complete; voluntarily participating; responding to questions with thorough responses; asking quality questions; etc. The X-axis is the teacher's judgment of how well the instructional practice was implemented based on knowledge of the practice, engagement of the student, or thoroughness of preparation. The judgment goes from –1.0, showing very little success with the practice, to a +1.0, which is extensive knowledge about the practice. Plotting strategies used on the grid can give teachers a picture of what is working in the classroom and why (see Table 12.2).

Table 12.2   Teacher Judgment on Implementation of Instructional Practice

Lucky	Leading
Losing	Learning

| –1.0 | –0.5 | 0 | +0.5 | +1.0 |

Reeves (2006) categorizes each quadrant (moving clockwise from the lower left quadrant): losing, lucky, leading, learning (p. 138). The losing practices are those that have little preparation and poor student results. These practices should be abandoned or the teacher should seek professional development. Lucky practices have little teacher understanding of the practice but high student results. These should be continued, but with more teacher preparation. Leading practices are those that are understood well by the teacher and consistently bring high student achievement. These should also be continued and shared with other teachers. Learning practices yield low student achievement, but the teacher is dedicated to their implementation and is continually gathering knowledge on the practice. It is possible that some learning practices are ineffective because the teacher is missing a key component of their implementation, and in this case, needs to gain additional support or knowledge.

A further step is to create focus groups based on practices teachers want to improve. Creating focus-question groups helps teachers explore concerns and makes further learning about single-gender education more meaningful. This procedure is described in Chapter 10.

Presenting at Conferences

Supporting and encouraging teachers to present at conferences builds a reputation for the school and requires teachers to reflect on their practice.

University Partnerships

Nearby colleges might be interested in collaborating with schools that have single-gender programs. Professors who teach child development or instructional practices may find single-gender classes an enrichment opportunity for their students. Professors may want to conduct site visitations, place student-teachers in single-gender classes, or have guest speakers for their lectures. The school benefits by having professors supply student-teachers or interns for their classes. The university may also provide professional development on an issue related to gender or how gender intersects with other aspects of teaching, or by assisting with research and assessment. A university partnership can also bring grant opportunities to support efforts at the school.

INSTITUTING CHANGE

Ken Blanchard, author of *Who Killed Change* (2009), suggests that there are thirteen factors that play a role in any successful organizational change: culture, commitment, sponsorship, change leadership team, communication, urgency, vision, planning, budget, trainer, incentive, performance management, and accountability (pp. 126–43). Attending to the thirteen factors of change is critical for sustaining a single-gender program and each factor has been addressed at some point within this book.

Incorporating a single-gender program into a school is a type of school reform. It needs the support, care, and patience of any reform model. But school single-gender education can be implemented quickly with little cost. This is critical as the demands of accountability loom over every public school teacher, student, and administrator. Meeting the needs of all children never ceases, and using gender is an additional tool for educators.

CHAPTER 12 PLANNING TOOL: SUSTAINING CHANGE

Use the categories and prompts below too help plan for a successful single-gender program. Eventually broaden the conversation to include parent organizations and teachers.

Leadership Factors for Successful Change

- How will you keep current with what is happening in the field of gender and single-gender education?

- How will you keep teachers excited and optimistic about single-gender education?

- How will you bring new research about single-gender education to teachers?

- How will you keep teachers focused on the goals of the single-gender program?

- How will you develop a system for monitoring the single-gender program?

- How will you know when to adjust the practices and policies of the single-gender program?

- How will you ensure that you are not sacrificing the key rationale for creating the single-gender program?

- How will you imbed the single-gender program into the description of your school?
  Newsletter
  School Web site
  Fax cover sheet
  School letterhead
  Parent sessions
  Other

- In what way will the whole staff be able to reflect on gender as an issue in their classrooms?
  Faculty meetings
  Lesson plans
  Small group meetings

Principal or leadership communications (message board, newsletters, announcements)
Professional development
Other

- When can teachers of single-gender classes meet?

- What will be the focus of these meetings?
Sharing strategies and observations
Discussion of student performance
Gathering and sharing research on gender
Gathering, sharing, and analyzing data
Planning of lessons and activities
Revision of program
Other

- How will teachers continue to receive professional development?
Book studies
Faculty meetings
Articles or chapters from texts
Sharing of practice
Reflection on practice
Mentoring of teachers
University partnerships
Other

- What level of commitment do you or your school leadership have to sustain a single-gender program? How will this support the development of your program? What needs to be done to develop solid support?

- What level of availability do you or your school leadership have to sustain a single-gender program? How will this support the development of your program? What needs to be done to provide adequate time?

- Who can help you or your school leadership to sustain your single-gender program? (You may want to refer to Chapter 10 on professional development for more ideas.)
School personnel
Parent support
Student support
District support
Community members
Regional members
University members
Professional organizations
National organizations
Other

Implementation Year	Development of Program	Tasks Involved in Development	Point Person Responsible	Monitoring Procedure
Year One				
Year Two				
Year Three				
Year Four				
Year Five				

Reproducible Resources

Resource A

Sample Creeds From Single-Sex Schools

1. Sample Creed From B.E.S.T. Academy for Boys, Atlanta, GA

I am a young man
Growing strong
Using my mind
To create words to fashion images, and to perform deeds.
I will respect myself and others
I promise to be and do my
BEST
Some day I may land short of my goals
But I will not fall
With the guidance of my teachers, family, friends, and the BEST Academy
I will live diligently each day knowing
I owe it to myself and the world to take full advantage of the vast opportunities
presented before me
That will shape my very existence
To continue to be the very
BEST I can be

2. Sample Creed From Killian Elementary School, Columbia, SC

Determined: "I can overcome any obstacle."

Inspired: "I am destined to be great."

Respected: "I am worthy of praise."

Excellent: "I never settle for less."

Culture: "I am a gentleman."

Talented: "I am gifted."

Intent: "I am focused and driven."

Open: "I am free from limitations."

Noble: "I display qualities of high moral character, honor, generosity, and courage."

Resource B

Sample Proposal Form for Creating a Single-Gender Program

GENERAL INFORMATION

School Name:

District:

Contact Person for Program:

Email for Contact Person:

RATIONALE

Rationale for Single-Gender Program (cite specific data from your school to support the need):

PROGRAM DETAILS

Single-Gender Grade Levels:

Single-Gender Subject Areas:

Specifics of the Structure:

SELECTION OF STUDENTS

Will students opt in or opt out?

If you are having students opt in, what will your criteria be for placement (lottery or objective criteria—please explain)?

If you are having students opt out, how will you identify students?

How will you communicate with parents that they have the option to opt out?

What is the minimum number of students you need in each class to make a single-gender class?

What is the maximum number of students that you will allow in a single-gender class?

Anticipated number of students participating:

Anticipated number of teachers participating:

COED OPTION

What is your plan for offering a coed option?

COMMUNICATION

Date of discussion with PTO/SIC:

Date of discussion with faculty:

Date of initial training of faculty members (should be by the end of the school year):

Date of parent meeting regarding gender differences and program specifics (should be before spring break):

PROFESSIONAL DEVELOPMENT

Proposed professional development during the year:

DATA COLLECTION

Planned data collection throughout the year:

Resource C

Sample Team-Building Activities for Students

TITLE OF ACTIVITY: BALL TOSS

Overview

Students gather in a circle and try to keep the ball in the air as long as possible and gain as many points as possible. Students keep the ball in the air by hitting it with their hands, head, or feet. The group receives 1 point for a hand hit, 2 points for a head hit, and 3 points for a foot hit. The only rules are that (1) the ball cannot touch the ground, walls, ceiling and the group starts over at zero if it does and (2) one person cannot hit the ball two times consecutively.

Materials

- Beach ball or similar inflatable ball (one per ten people)
- Strips of paper with the name of each student (for selection of leader)
- Space to hit the ball in the air—outside is ideal

Procedure

1. Explain the purpose of ball toss.

2. Give students five minutes to brainstorm strategy.

3. Have students determine their strategy. You may want to randomly assign a leader for a specific number of attempts and then rotate leaders.

4. Give the ball to the leader.

5. Leader starts by hitting the ball. (Teacher counts the points.)

6. The round continues with students hitting the ball and gathering points.

7. The round ends when the ball hits a wall, ground, ceiling, or a student hits the ball two times consecutively.

8. Give the leader a chance to process as necessary (or change leaders).

9. Start another round.

When to Use

Ball toss is used as a team-building activity. Do this activity during the beginning of the year and periodically throughout the year. One ball toss session typically lasts ten minutes. Students, particularly boys, will hit the ball as hard as possible in the beginning. They will run all over the field chasing the ball. They will yell at each other to get it or make comments about mistakes. Some will not participate at all. Let all of this happen.

Later, talk with the students about their decisions. Are they effective? Are they reaching their goal? They will bring up the idea of listening, calling for the ball, and probably not hitting the ball too hard. They may also decide to arrange themselves in a different form and that is fine. At some point, talk with the students about how their behavior during ball toss probably mirrors their behavior during group projects in the classroom. Help the students make the connection that each student acting out his or her own desires will not help the group achieve their goal.

Rationale

Ball toss is a highly physical activity that gives students a forum to experience and talk about group dynamics. Students, particularly boys, are moving in a structured and planned way and are able to use their experience to draw connections to classroom behavior.

TITLE OF ACTIVITY: FRIENDSHIP

Overview

Students role-play friendship situations to demonstrate how the situations get worse and get better. It is a proactive way to address friendship concerns.

Materials

- Index cards
- Poster paper

Procedures

1. Have students write down a situation in which they got angry with another person or friend. They can use made-up names or letters (e.g., "X").

2. Categorize the situations into groups and label each group. This can be done as a separate activity with the students or by the teacher.

3. Determine which category should be role-played first. Again, the teacher can decide or the students can vote or have input.

4. Select one situation to have students role-play and prepare hand-outs for students to read. The handout is an edited version of the situations submitted by the students.

5. Have one group of students role-play the situation getting worse and another group of students role-play the situation getting better.

6. While the students are role-playing the situations, the teacher and the other students write down the trigger words, actions, shrugs, etc. that make the situation better or worse.

7. These lists are posted for students to see. The teacher can refer to them as well, during different moments within the class.

8. Process the role-playing in small groups, as a whole class, or individually as necessary.

9. Continue role-playing with new situations every two weeks.

When to Use

The friendship activity should be used once a week or every other week to address typical and potential friendship concerns. When there are conflicts within the class, the teacher can refer students to the list to help them understand that there is a reason why the situation got worse and recommend ways to improve.

Rationale

The friendship activity tends to work well because the situations come from the students themselves.

Resource D

Organizations for the Learning of Boys and Girls

Center for the Study of Boys' and Girls' Lives
www.csbl.org

Chadwell Consulting
www.chadwellconsulting.com

Coalition of Schools Educating Boys of Color
www.coseboc.org

The Deak Group
www.deakgroup.com

Diplomas Count 2008 by *Education Week*
www.edweek.org/ew/toc/2008/06/05

Girls Inc. and Supergirl Dilemma
www.girlsincholyoke.org/about-us/supergirl-dilemma-report

The Gurian Institute
www.gurianinstitute.org

International Boys School Coalition
www.theibsc.org

National Association for Single-Sex Public Education
www.nasspe.org

National Coalition of Girls' Schools
www.ncgs.org

Rockhouse Associates
www.rockhouseassociates.org

Rosalind Wiseman
www.rosalindwiseman.com

Schott Foundation
www.blackboysreport.org

Resource E

Sample Annual Single-Gender
Program Review Form

Principal:

Assistant Principal:

The following review must be completed by a school that has a single-gender program during the school year. All thirteen questions must be answered. It is recommended that the school send the review to the district superintendent and share results with teachers and the parent community.

General Information

1. School Name:

2. District Name:

3. Name of Person Completing Review:

4. Email of Person Completing Review:

5. Telephone Number of Person Completing Review:

Demographic Information

6. Please indicate the number of girl (G) and boy (B) classes in each subject area and grade level within your school.

	ELA	Math	SCI	SS	Art	PE	Tech	Media	Music	Other
K Girl										
K Boy										
1st G										
1st B										
2nd G										
2nd B										
3rd G										
3rd B										
4th G										
4th B										
5th G										
5th B										
6th G										
6th B										
7th G										
7th B										
8th G										
8th B										
9th G										
9th B										
10th G										
10th B										
11th G										
11th B										
12th G										
12th B										

7. Please indicate the number of *students* [girls (G) and boys (B)] in each subject area and grade level within your school.

	ELA	Math	SCI	SS	Art	PE	Tech	Media	Music	Other
K Girl										
K Boy										
1st G										
1st B										
2nd G										
2nd B										
3rd G										
3rd B										
4th G										
4th B										
5th G										
5th B										
6th G										
6th B										
7th G										
7th B										
8th G										
8th B										
9th G										
9th B										
10th G										
10th B										
11th G										
11th B										
12th G										
12th B										

Program Rationale

8. Please indicate the rationale for creating a single-gender program at your school. (Please mark with an "X"—mark all that apply.)

Increased Choice Options for Parents and Students

Increased Academic Achievement for Students

Decreased Discipline Referrals

Increased Attendance Rate

Increased Graduation Rate

Decreased Dropout Rate

Improved Student Self-Concept

Increased Student Participation

Decreased Student Gender Stereotypes

Closing the Achievement Gap

Other:

Review of Single-Gender Program

9. In your own words, how effective was the single-gender program in meeting the indicated rationales? You must provide a statement for each of the rationales indicated in question #8.

10. Overall, to what degree did the single-gender program meet its expectations? (Please mark with an "X"—select one.)

Exceeded Expectations

Fully Met Expectations

Partially Met Expectations

Did Not Meet Expectations—No Change in Performance

Did Not Meet Expectations—Negative Impact on Student Performance

11. Please include data that support your conclusions about your single-gender program. Your data should reflect your indicated rationales and should include gendered subgroups (ethnic and racial subgroups would also be helpful). The following form can be used, but is not required:

Data Set	Term	Gender	Race	Type of Class	Data	Comments
Indicate the name of the data that you are using (i.e., below basic on standardized test, in-school suspensions, tardies, or graduation rate).	Indicate the time frame or term of the data: year, month, quarter of information (i.e., 2007–2008 school year, fall semester 2007).	Indicate which gender is included in the data: female, male, or both.	Indicate which race is included in the data: African American, Asian American, Caucasian, Hispanic, other, all.	Indicate if the students were in coed classes (CE) or single-gender classes (SG).	The actual raw data (number) (i.e., percent, count).	Comment, interpretation, or significance of data.

Plan for Next Year

12. What is your intention for the next school year? (Please mark with an "X"—select one.)

Continue the single-gender program in the same grades and subject areas; please indicate what this will be:

Expand the single-gender program to include additional grades or subject areas; please indicate:

Reduce the single-gender program in the following grades or subject areas; please explain new format and reason for change:

Terminate the single-gender program; please explain reason:

13. What is your plan for improving the single-gender program for the next school year?

Resource F

Sample Letter to Parents to Survey Their Interest

This is a sample Parent-Interest Survey Letter to be used to determine if parents are interested in their child participating in a single-gender program.

Dear Parents,

As you are aware, we have been considering ways to continue our mission of academic excellence. We are considering creating single-gender classes in Grades X–X. As a community, we have been learning more about the differences between boys and girls and how we can better meet their needs in the classroom. We have been in communication with teachers, parents, and the district administration. We appreciate the terrific support we have received thus far.

We are excited about the possibility of this type of program. The benefits of single-gender classes have been discussed in a multitude of research articles and our teachers have even noted some of the immediate benefits that they would expect at our school. Here's how this might look:

> **Teacher A would teach a class of approximately 23 girls during the morning, while Teacher B taught a class of approximately 23 boys. Students would have lunch, PE, and most likely recess together. In the afternoon, Teacher B would teach the girls while the boys went to Teacher A.**

Before we consider proceeding with this schedule, we would like to conduct a Parent-Interest Survey. If you are not familiar with the research on single-gender classes, we encourage you to search the Internet or visit the library to read about this topic. We will also offer a parent information night on XX. Please take a moment to complete the survey below and return it to the main office by XX.

Respectfully,

_____ I would be comfortable with my child being assigned to single-gender classes.
_____ I would like more information about single-gender education.
_____ I do not want my child to be assigned to single-gender classes.

Child's Name	Parent/Guardian Signature

Resource G

Sample Letter to Parents Informing Them of Single–Gender Program and Surveying Their Interest

This is a sample parent interest letter to inform parents about the school's intention to offer single-gender classes and to determine parent interest.

Dear Parent or Guardian:

TERRIFIC School District is embarking on a new and exciting educational opportunity for our children. The educational opportunity is single-gender classes for students in the X grade. Our children learn the same content and standards, but may take different paths in the learning process. Research shows that single-gender classrooms can increase the student's opportunity. Listed below are some facts from the research.

Typical Benefits for Girls	Typical Benefits for Boys
o More interest in and enthusiasm for math and science	o Better chance of being on the college preparatory road
o More academically inclined	o More development of reading and writing skills
o More time on task in the classroom	o Better chance of not dropping out of high school
o More open to discuss sensitive issues and concerns	o More focused participation
o More interest in classroom participation	o More open to discuss issues and concerns
o More likely to study more advanced levels of mathematics and science	o More opportunity to learn collaborative working strategies
o More likely to accept and develop leadership roles	o Fewer gender distractions
o Fewer gender distractions	o Less likely to have stereotypical view of females
o Less likely to have stereotypical views of females in the workplace	o More likely to develop a positive attitude toward school
o More enjoyment of school	

Please help us in planning for this new opportunity by completing the survey below. Please return the survey before XX.

If you have questions about single-gender classes, you may contact me at XX.

✂ --

Student Name: _____   Gender: Male or Female

Current School _____

    ❑ I am interested in my child participating in single-gender classes.

    ❑ I am not interested in my child participating in single-gender classes.

    ❑ I would like more information about single-gender classes. Contact: _____

    ❑ I would like to discuss single-gender classes with the principal. Contact: _____

Parent Name: _____

Resource H

Sample Letter to Parents (School Selecting Students With Coed Option Explained)

This is a Sample Parent Letter to inform them of single-gender classes and *the school* will select the students. A coed choice is explained.

Dear Parents,

We are excited to announce the start of a single-gender program at TERRIFIC School. This program continues the tradition of excellence and innovation at TERRIFIC School. Single-gender education is being adopted by many schools and districts across the country as a way of providing choices for parents and alternative learning environments for students. Recent brain research shows that there are important differences between boys and girls that can impact the learning environment and the ways that teachers teach. Teachers, parents, and students who participate in single-gender classes have been very enthusiastic and positive about their programs.

Your child has been selected to participate in our program. While not all students are able to benefit from single-gender classes at this time, we believe your child is ideally suited to take advantage of this opportunity. Your child will have single-gender classes in the following areas: *list areas*.

The teachers are preparing for an outstanding year. Your child's success is at the heart of all decisions made at TERRIFIC School. I appreciate your continued support for TERRIFIC School and the programs we offer our students. You have the option of having your child placed in coed classes if you choose. The coed choice would be XX. Please contact me with any questions regarding this program.

I look forward to another great year at TERRIFIC School.

Resource I

Sample Letter to Parents (All Students in Single-Gender With Coed Option Explained)

This is a Sample Parent Letter to inform parents that single-gender classes will be instituted. All students will be in single-gender classes. A coed option is explained.

DATE

Dear Parents/Guardians,

Please let me preface this letter by saying that I look forward to having your son/daughter at TERRIFIC School starting XX. TERRIFIC School will be your child's home away from home. And, my goal is to do everything within my power to make him or her feel like a vital member of the TERRIFIC School team.

TERRIFIC School has a history in providing the best educational opportunities for its students. Over the years, we have instituted several outstanding educational programs. This year, looking at learning styles and classroom discipline, we have decided to have single-gender classes (classes with all boys and all girls) for this year's X-grade core classes. We are excited about the opportunities for increased learning and decreased distractions. Students will be mixed during their elective classes.

We are happy to say that our school board has approved the decision of allowing us to have X- grade single-gender classes this upcoming school year.

Please keep in mind that as decisions are made, students' achievement and success is at the core of any changes being made. This is no different. We anticipate success from this change and look forward to a wonderful school year. Of course, you have the choice to have your child participate in coed classes. Those coed classes would exist XX.

Please feel free to give me a call at XX or email me at XX with any questions or concerns.

Sincerely yours,

References

Adcox, S. (2007, October 1) S.C. at forefront of single-gender classes. *Boston Globe*. Retrieved from http://www.boston.com/news/nation/articles/2007/10/01/sc_at_forefront_of_single_gender_classes/?rss_id=Boston+Globe+—+National+News.

American Association of University Women. (2008). Where the women are. *The Facts about Gender Equity and Education Executive Summary*. Washington, DC: Author.

American Civil Liberties Union [ACLU]. (2007). *Single-sex education*. Retrieved from the ACLU Web site http://www.aclu.org/womensrights/edu/30129 res20070614.html.

American Civil Liberties Union [ACLU]. (2008). *About the women's rights project education*. Retrieved from the ACLU Web site http://www.aclu.org/womensrights/index.html.

Armstrong, T. (2006). *The best schools: How human development research should inform educational practice*. Alexandria, VA: Association for Supervision and Curriculum Development.

Banchero, S. (2006, November 5). Boys in one class, girls in the other. *Chicago Tribune*. Retrieved from http://archives.chicagotribune.com/2006/nov/05/news/chi-0611050367nov05.

Barnett, R., & Rivers, C. (2004). *Same difference*. New York: Basic Books.

Baron-Cohen, S. (2003). *The essential difference: The truth about the male and female brain*. New York: Basic Books.

Blanchard, K. (2009). *Who killed change?* New York: HarperCollins.

Blum, D. (1997). *Sex on the brain*. New York: Penguin Books.

Bracey, G. (2006). *Separate but superior? A review of issues and data bearing on single-sex education*. East Lansing, MI: The Great Lakes Center for Education Research and Practice.

Brizendine, L. (2006). *The female brain*. New York: Morgan Road Books.

Dart, A., Du, X., & Kingwell, B. (2002). Gender, sex hormones and autonomic nervous control of the cardiovascular system. *Cardiovascular Research*, 53(3), 678–687. Retrieved from http://cardiovascres.oxfordjournals.org/cgi/content/full/53/3/678.

Datnow, A., Hubbard, L., & Woodly, E. (2001). *Is single gender schooling viable in the public sector? Lessons from California's pilot program*. Retrieved from http://www.oise.utoronto.ca/depts/tps/adatnow/final.pdf.

Deak, J. (2002). *Girls will be girls*. New York: Hyperion.

Dewey, J. (1916). *Democracy and education: An introduction to the philosophy of education*. New York: The MacMillan Company.

Education Week. (2008). Diplomas count 2008. Retrieved from http://www.edweek.org/ew/toc/2008/06/05/index.html.

Eliot, L., & Bailey, S. (2008, August 20). Gender segregation in the schools isn't the answer. *USA Today*. Retrieved from http://blogs.usatoday.com/oped/2008/08/gender-segregat.html.

Federal Register. (2006). Nondiscrimination on the basis of sex in education programs or activities receiving federal financial assistance; Final rule. Retrieved from http://www.ed.gov/legislation/FedRegister/finrule/2006–4/102506a.html.

Fletcher, R. (2006). *Boy writers: Reclaiming their voices.* Portland, ME: Stenhouse.

Gabriel, J. (2005). *How to thrive as a teacher leader.* Alexandria, VA: Association for Supervision and Curriculum Development.

Gender Matters, South Carolina Department of Education, Public School Choice Single-Gender Initiative, Single-Gender Newsletters. August 2007, October 2007, January 2008, April 2008, August 2008. Retrieved September 7, 2008, from http://www.ed.sc.gov/agency/Innovation-and-Support/Public-School-Choice/SingleGender/SingleGenderNewsletters.html.

Ginsberg, A., Shapiro, J., & Brown, S. (2004). *Gender in urban education.* Portsmouth, NH: Heinemann.

Gurian, M. (2001). *Boys and girls learn differently!* San Francisco: Jossey-Bass.

Gurian, M., & Stevens, K. (2005). *The minds of boys.* San Francisco: Jossey-Bass.

Hall, J. (1984). *Nonverbal sex differences: Communication accuracy and expressive style.* Baltimore, MD: Johns Hopkins University Press.

Hines, M. (2004). *Brain gender.* New York: Oxford University Press.

Illinois State Report Card. (2007). Retrieved from http://webprod.isbe.net/ereportcard/publicsite/getReport.aspx?year=2007&code=2007StateReport_E.pdf.

James, A. (2007). *Teaching the male brain.* Thousand Oaks, CA: Corwin.

James, A. (2009). *Teaching the female brain.* Thousand Oaks, CA: Corwin.

Jensen, E. (2000). *Brain-based learning.* San Diego, CA: The Brain Store.

Jensen, E. (2006). *Enriching the brain: How to maximize every learner's potential.* San Francisco: Jossey-Bass.

Kepner, A. (2008, January 12). Lawmakers' bill supports all-boys charter middle school. *The News Journal.* Retrieved from http://www.delawareonline.com.

Kimura, D. (1999). *Sex and cognition.* Cambridge, MA: MIT Press.

Kissell, M. (2005, January 15). Officials support same-sex schools. *Dayton Daily News,* pp. B1, B4.

Klein, G., & Owens, D. (2006, April 9). At S.C. school, a rising tide of achievement. *Richmond Times-Dispatch,* p. A8.

Lim, S. (2007, August 26). Closing the gender gap in Manatee schools. *Bradenton Herald,* p. 1A.

Maccoby, E. (Ed.) (1966). *The development of sex differences.* Stanford, CA: Stanford University Press.

Marzano, R., Waters, T., & McNulty, B. (2005). *School leadership that works.* Alexandria, VA: Association for Supervision and Curriculum Development.

Meyer, P. (2008, Winter). Learning separately: The case for single-sex schools. *Education Next.* Retrieved from www.educationnext.org.

National Organization for Women. (2008). *NOW and single-sex education.* Retrieved from http://www.now.org/issues/education/single-sex-education.html.

Newkirk, T. (2002). *Misreading masculinity: Boys, literacy, and popular culture.* Portsmouth, NH: Heinemann.

New York State Report Card. (2007). Retrieved from https://www.nystart.gov/publicweb-external/2007statewideAOR.pdf.

Noguera, P. (2008). *The trouble with black boys . . . and other reflections on race, equity, and the future of public education.* San Francisco: Jossey-Bass.

Nosek, B., et al. (2009). National differences in gender-science stereotypes predict national sex differences in science and math achievement. *Proceedings of the National Academy of Sciences,* 106 (26), 10593–10597. Retrieved from http://www.pnas.org/content/106/26/10593.

Pinkner, S. (2008). *The sexual paradox: Men, women, and the real gender gap.* New York: Scribner.

Pollack, W. (1999). *Real Boys.* New York: Henry Holt and Company.

Reeves, D. (2006). *The learning leader: How to focus school improvement for better results.* Alexandria, VA: Association for Supervision and Curriculum Development.

Rimm, S. (1999). *See Jane win: The Rimm Report on how 1,000 girls became successful women.* New York: Crown.

Salomone, R. (2002). *Same, different, equal: Rethinking single-sex schooling.* New Haven, CT: Yale University Press.

Sax, L. (2005). *Why gender matters.* New York: Basic Books.

Silva, E. (2008, March 16). Boys and girls are more alike in school than they are different. *Delaware News Journal.* Retrieved from http://www.educationsector.org/analysis/analysis_show.htm?doc_id=673669.

Simmons, R. (2002). *Odd girl out.* Orlando, FL: Harcourt.

Slocumb, P. (2004). *Hear our cry: Boys in crisis.* Highlands, TX: Aha! Process Inc.

Sousa, D. (2006). *How the brain learns.* Thousand Oaks, CA: Corwin.

South Carolina Department of Education (2005–2008). *South Carolina State Report Card.* Retrieved from http://www.ed.sc.gov/topics/researchandstats/schoolreportcard.

South Carolina Department of Education. (2008). *South Carolina surveys on single-gender education, July 2008.* Retrieved from http://www.ed.sc.gov/agency/Innovation-and-Support/Public-School-Choice/SingleGender/Documents/FINALSouthCarolinaSingleGenderSurveyReportMay2008.pdf.

Tomlinson, C. A. (2001). *How to differentiate instruction in mixed-ability classrooms.* Alexandria, VA: Association for Supervision and Curriculum Development.

Tomlinson, C. A. (2003). *Fulfilling the promise of the differentiated classroom.* Alexandria, VA: Association for Supervision and Curriculum Development.

Tyre, P. (2008). *Trouble with boys.* New York: Crown.

United States v. Virginia et al., 518 U.S. 515 (U.S. Court of Appeals for the 4th Circuit, 1996).

U.S. Department of Education, Institute of Education Sciences, National Center for Education Statistics, National Assessment of Educational Progress (NAEP). *1992, 1994, 1998, 2000, 2002, 2003, 2005 and 2007 Reading Assessments* [data file]. Available from http://nces.ed.gov/nationsreportcard.

U.S. Department of Education, Institute of Education Sciences, National Center for Education Statistics, National Assessment of Educational Progress (NAEP). *1990, 1992, 1996, 2000, 2003, 2005 and 2007 Mathematics Assessments* [data file]. Available from http://nces.ed.gov/nationsreportcard.

U.S. Department of Education, Institute of Education Sciences, National Center for Education Statistics, National Assessment of Educational Progress (NAEP). (2008). *The NAEP Glossary of Terms.* Retrieved from http://nces.ed.gov/nationsreportcard/glossary.asp#top.

U.S. Department of Education, Office of Planning, Evaluation and Policy Development, Policy and Program Studies Service. (2005). *Single-sex versus secondary schooling: A systematic review.* Washington, DC: Author. Retrieved from http://www.ed.gov/about/offices/list/opepd/reports.html.

U.S. Department of Labor. *Title IX, Education Amendments of 1972.* Retrieved from http://www.dol.gov/oasam/regs/statutes/titleix.htm.

Vaznis, J. (2008, October 29). School revamp hits a snag. *Boston Globe.* Retrieved from http://www.boston.com/news/education/k_12/articles/2008/10/29/school_revamp_hits_a_snag.

Wack, K., Quimby, B., & Menendez, J. (2006, March 26). Boys in jeopardy at school. *Maine Sunday Telegram.* Retrieved from http://pressherald.mainetoday.com/specialrpts/boys/060326boys.shtml.

Washington State Report Card. (2007). Retrieved from http://reportcard.ospi.k12.wa.us/WASLCurrent.aspx?schoolId=1&reportLevel=State&year=2007–08&gradeLevelId=3&groupLevel=District&waslCategory=3&chartType=2.

Weil, E. (2008). Should boys and girls be taught separately? *New York Times Magazine.* March, 38–45, 84–87.

Wilhelm, J. (2002). *Action strategies for deepening comprehension.* New York: Scholastic.

Yes, university women, there is a boy problem. [Editorial]. (2008, May 21). *USA Today.* Retrieved from http://www.usatoday.com/printedition/news/20080521/edit21.art.htm.

Index

CORWIN
A SAGE Company

The Corwin logo—a raven striding across an open book—represents the union of courage and learning. Corwin is committed to improving education for all learners by publishing books and other professional development resources for those serving the field of PreK–12 education. By providing practical, hands-on materials, Corwin continues to carry out the promise of its motto: **"Helping Educators Do Their Work Better."**